The Bible as Dream:
A Jungian Interpretation

Murray Stein

PUBLISHED BY CHIRON PUBLICATIONS

www.ChironPublications.com

Interior and cover design by Danijela Mijailovic
Printed primarily in the United States of America.

ISBN 978-1-63051-668-0 paperback
ISBN 978-1-63051-669-7 hardcover
ISBN 978-1-63051-670-3 electronic
ISBN 978-1-63051-671-0 limited edition paperback

Library of Congress Cataloging-in-Publication Data

Names: Stein, Murray, 1943- author.
Title: The Bible as dream : a Jungian interpretation / Murray Stein.
Description: Asheville : Chiron Publications, 2018. | Includes
    bibliographical references and index.
Identifiers: LCCN 2018041705 | ISBN 9781630516680 (pbk. :
    alk. paper) | ISBN 9781630516697 (hardcover : alk. paper)
Subjects: LCSH: Bible--Criticism, interpretation, etc. | Bible--
    Psychology. | Psychoanalysis and religion. | Jungian psychology.
    | Dreams--Religious aspects--Christianity.
Classification: LCC BS645 .S74 2018 | DDC 220.601/9--dc23
LC record available at https://lccn.loc.gov/2018041705

TABLE OF CONTENTS

Acknowledgments

The lectures on "A Psychological Reading of the Bible" were delivered in February, 1989 at the Jung Center in Evanston, Illinois. The lectures on "The Gospel of John" were given at the Catholic Seminary in Mundelein, Illinois in the summer of 1989. I wish to thank the students and others in attendance at these lectures for their patience and supportive reception. The lectures were an attempt to isolate some important themes and images in the biblical narrative that from a psychological perspective stand out as essential features of the meaning that the Bible conveys to a modern reader. My teachers in this approach were above all C.G. Jung and his famous students such as Erich Neumann, Marie-Louise von Franz, Rivkah Kluger, and Joseph Henderson. I also owe an enormous debt of gratitude to my professors at Yale Divinity School, especially to Paul Schubert, Professor of New Testament. Their love of the Scriptures was inspiring and endearing. Finally, to my father, Walter Stein, whose ministry was centered on teaching the Bible to his parishioners and his children, and to my mother, Jeanette Stein, who was as dedicated a Sunday School teacher as has ever been known. By all of these people my life has been blessed and my mind enriched.

PART I

A Psychological Reading of the Bible

On Reading the Bible Psychologically

The Interpreter

The Bible is a world elaborated with reference to a specific God image, Yahweh. As the mythographer Karl Kerenyi puts it in writing about the Greek gods and goddesses, every god and every goddess constitutes a world. So it is too with the biblical God, whose name I will exceptionally capitalize throughout out of cultural respect.

The biblical world is the visionary product of a particular people, the ancient Hebrews and the early Christians, who delved deeply into their God image and pulled from it the multitude of perspectives, rules for life, spiritual practices, and other implications that all together created the tapestry that we find represented in the canonical Bible. Yahweh is the heart and soul of this world, its creator, sustainer, and destroyer. The Bible is His story and the story of how this world was brought into being in space and time and what it means.

In these lectures, I am offering a work of interpretation. Before beginning and asking you to consider my thoughts about the Bible, I need to let you know something about myself, the interpreter. An interpretation is shaped critically by the personal bias and interests of the author. It is different from a work of pure scholarship that attempts to be objective about its subject. Interpretation is an essay in understanding, or a kind of meditation. Without some minimal knowledge of the author, however, the reader cannot really estimate the value of the interpretation. You want to know where the author is coming from, what is the angle of their vision, what is their personal bias. Do I love the object I am interpreting, do I hate it, am I promoting it, or what?

I grew up in a Protestant parsonage. My father, a German immigrant, was a Baptist minister, and as a family we attended church three times a week: Sunday mornings for an hour of Sunday School and an hour of worship, Sunday evenings for an hour of hymn singing and sermonizing, and Wednesday evenings for an hour of Bible study. Bible School, which took place during summer vacations and went on for three weeks, was a given. In my youth I memorized large portions of the Bible and recited them by heart in front of the congregation. As fledgling students of the Scripture, we were awarded medals for these feats of memorization, and I earned several.

At home, our daily routines began as well with biblical content. Before breakfast every morning my mother would read a Bible story aloud from a big picture book. The Bible was omnipresent in my early years. I grew to know it well, and its authority and truthfulness were unquestioned. I grew up in the biblical world, and it was more familiar to me than the geographical worlds we inhabited as we moved from place to place every five years or so.

I vividly remember listening to a radio program called "The Greatest Story Ever Told." The entire Bible was treated as a single great story. The series dramatized episodes in this extended story and featured characters and scenes from the Bible. God's own bass voice was delivered with special effects to indicate His supernatural status. I remember feeling quite awestruck by some of the episodes. They were highly emotional – miracles of healing and deliverance. In every episode God would play a major role, sometimes directly by intervening in the narrative or otherwise indirectly by inspiring, instructing, or influencing the course of the action through dreams and visions. The great heroes of the Bible are characters especially tuned in to God's directives. This radio show gave one the feeling of having actually entered into the biblical world.

Eventually it occurred to me that the Bible is mainly about God and how people relate to Him. While there are many human protagonists, there is only one God. It is the same single God who is portrayed throughout the text. The Bible is this specific God's story.

At college and Divinity School, I studied the Bible in more formal scholarly ways with remarkable, gifted teachers. Reading the New Testament in the original Greek was a moving experience for me. I felt closer to the source, even though few of the biblical characters actually spoke in Greek or could have read the Greek text themselves. Textual criticism and form criticism left their marks on my awareness of the Bible world, as in my education I repeated the history of belief and faith from ancient times through the Middle Ages and Enlightenment down to the modern scientific age. Most decisively, I was introduced also to other world religions and their sacred scriptures, and in this I soon realized that the Bible world is not so singularly privileged. There are many sacred texts, many divinely structured worlds, and all of them have wisdom to offer. Finally, the discovery of Jung and his writings on theological and biblical themes opened the way to the approach I am taking in these lectures.

Concerning Interpretation

The Bible I grew up with is a story of the history of the world from its very beginnings, when God created everything that exists in six days, to its ending, when God will pass His final judgment and ring down the curtain. But after an early point, it is focused primarily on the history of one group of people: the ancient Hebrews and their Christian descendants. A highly significant aspect of the overall story is how these people dealt with their God and how they went about living their lives with a religious attitude. The human ideal, as represented by such key figures as Abraham, Sarah, Moses, Ruth, David, the prophets, Jesus, Mary, Paul, and many others, is the continuous conscious submission to God's will. Faith in and obedience to God are seen as the supreme human virtues in the Bible.

If you study and live with the Bible as I did as a child and as we together did as a family, the history of the Bible and the characters in it become your own kinsfolk. You enter into the biblical world in an imaginative way. I actually felt very close to figures like Moses, David, Jesus, Peter, and Paul. They did not seem like strange or distant people, historically or culturally. There was a kind of collapse of time and cultural distance in the way the Bible was presented and lived in our churchly circle. We also felt present to God Himself by staying so closely connected to a text that was proclaimed as His Holy Word. The sacred history of God's people became our history, their miracles our miracles, their joys and sufferings ours as well. It was a leap of imagination and psychological identification that made all of this so familiar – so our own. The Bible provided the central reference point for our individual and group identity, located though we were on the stark prairieland of North Dakota so many thousands of miles and thousands of years away from the times and places described in the biblical narrative. In a sense we lived in two worlds: the biblical and the actual.

This type of familiarity did not mean that the Bible became a commonplace book on the shelf. People feel awe in the presence of God, and because the Bible was taken to be His own words it also had a sacred aura about it. Simply holding the book in one's hand inspires solemn reverence. When taking the oath of office, the President of the United States places his right hand on the Bible and vows to the people that he will uphold the laws of the land. This gives his words gravity. He cannot take the oath of office lightly if he swears by the Holy Bible. In court the ordinary citizen is asked to place a hand on the Bible, raise the other, and swear to tell the whole truth and nothing but the truth. The Bible seals the covenant and backs up the promises made on these solemn occasions. So one becomes especially serious around the biblical text.

This is a sacred text. It has been protected zealously by generations of believers and defended by brilliant theologians and by ordinary men and women of faith. Even if one does not accept the claim that this book is the undiluted Word of God, the aura of authority surrounding it remains impressive. One does not handle this text lightly. Considered as the written Word of God, the Bible itself is numinous. Granted that the present age is generally described as secular, the Bible nevertheless remains a sacred and privileged text for many people. One must respect it. It is a book that has provided a clear and steady compass for the spirit of generations of men and women in their search for truth and meaning. It has nourished their souls. This was certainly true in my own family of origin.

It is therefore with some fear and trembling that I approach the task of interpreting the Bible from a psychological point of view. I take some comfort in knowing that every reading of the Bible is an interpretation. Even the most literal understanding is based on a stated or assumed theory of interpretation. My mother reading the Bible to me at breakfast communicated and assumed things about the text. We would often discuss the implications of the stories for our own lives, seeking out spiritual and moral lessons and bringing them into play. Rabbis, the most careful and respectful of all interpreters of the Bible, have said that every word of the Bible can be understood in thirty-eight ways! There cannot be only one true interpretation of it. The sheer act of reading this text aloud in a public worship service, for instance, is an act of interpretation, a statement about its meaning. To draw lessons for life from the stories of the Bible, as ministers do in their sermons every Sunday, involves interpretation. Studying the Bible as literature in a secular university classroom or as a historical document in the study of ancient Near Eastern religions implies interpretation. Interpretation is the act of making a text intelligible from a certain angle of vision. No text, let alone one as complex and full of riddles as the Bible, is so transparent that its intended meaning simply shines through.

Some interpretations, however, reduce or demean a text, claiming that it is nothing but a disguise for something else and thus a fake or a delusion. Such interpretations actually attack the text and seek to dismember it and rob it of its power. A Marxist might read the Bible, for example, as a political tool to enslave the masses and to gain power over their labor. Other interpretations elevate and idealize a text, adding to its own claims of specialness. Every interpretation, however, represents a point of view on the text. It is impossible to interpret a text without leaving something out, without overvaluing and undervaluing some of its passages, without in other words distorting the text to some extent. I hope that the present interpretation will walk a line between the extremes. I want to show due respect even though I will be translating the text into a set of understandings that move the center of authority and gravity from the text itself. I do not mean to deconstruct the text, and yet an interpretation must have that effect to some extent. I will not claim to be speaking the ultimate truth about the text, but will rather seek to offer a way of seeing and reading it.

So what we have before us is a sacred text. Let's begin by asking a question that really cannot be answered definitively but does open up the discussion to an anthropological perspective: Why do sacred texts exist at all? The Bible is not unique in this respect. Sacred texts can be found universally, wherever there is a written language. Where language is not written down, sacred stories and doctrines are passed on and preserved in poems and oral forms that are recited from generation to generation by priests and teachers with near perfect memories. Every religious tradition claims a sacred story, or set of received doctrines and teachings, or collection of myths. Sacred texts exist because people need to honor the revelations of wisdom and the Divine. There is a need to preserve them and to learn lessons from them for daily life. They are soul food.

People revere and cherish their sacred stories and doctrines because the images and teachings in them are needed to establish and maintain a culture, its precise customs, and its patterns of collective behavior. Group identity depends on a shared myth.

Human beings are gifted and cursed with a very loosely organized instinctual system. Humans cannot rely on instinct to know what to do in everyday situations, especially those that involve other people. Consciously articulated cultural rules for living have therefore had to be instilled through indoctrination and education. Culture would be impossible without such norms. Once these norms and rules are encoded in sacred texts, constitutions, Bills of Rights, etc., they become "written in stone." That is, they assume the power and authority that instinct has in the rest of the animal world. The laws and customs of culture compensate for the lack of instinctual patterning that would tell us what to do in the variety of situations that we confront in everyday life. Myths organize human drives; archetypal images, as represented in story and myth, give specific form to basic human impulses. A sacred text plays this organizing role with supreme authority.

Texts, like the Bible, dimly, and sometimes only indirectly, reflect nature's own primordial rulebook: the instincts. The norms of society and human culture cannot be totally contradictory to nature. If they were, the species would not survive. But the range of possible solutions to the problems of knowing what to do with our energy and imagination and capacity for invention and play is vast. Cultures and societies are incredibly diverse in their preferences, customs, and practices. The variety of human behavior is phenomenal. Consider only one aspect: dress. In one culture, women bind their feet and wear the tiniest slippers possible. In another they wear no shoes at all but find nose rings de rigueur. In some cultures, men dress in feathers and shave their heads. In others they wear clothes made of the finest and most expensive fabrics and wear their hair long. None of these customs are necessarily more essentially human than the others. Some seem to foster and encourage general human growth and wellbeing more than others, and certainly from a modern Western point of view it seems that a society's customs and norms should not twist fundamental human patterns beyond the limit of what is psychically and physically healthy and natural. Otherwise individuals, if indeed they survive, will suffer extremely stunted and stultified lives. It must be said that sacred texts can be interpreted to mean things that are terribly harmful to some elements of the population.

The Bible belongs to a particular religious and cultural tradition. It reflects the ancient Hebrew and the later Christian forms of culture with their specific rules, regulations, and patterns of belief and behavior. There is nothing absolutely definitive about the cultural preferences described in the Bible. Many of the rules and customs no longer pertain to human life as it is lived in modern times. For instance, there is no need today to segregate lepers from the community. They can be treated by modern medicine in hospitals and sent home to their families. Stoning is no longer accepted as a just punishment for breaking the code of behavior in modern societies. If the Bible is the Word of God, it is so only in that it represents the way in which a specific people heard and interpreted His message and then worked out a set of rules that seemed to be in accordance with His will. Modern people tend to disagree with many of the details. So the Bible can and does speak of what is timeless and eternal, but it also discloses a world that is temporal and limited.

The Bible is therefore a mixture of the human and the divine. It represents a specific perspective on the divine and gives it an image. That is to say, the Bible is about a God image and not directly about God per se. It is about how a certain ancient people received and understood what they believed to be an experience of the Divine. Like all cultural artifacts, it is culture specific and limited by the knowledge and perspectives available to the people of the time in which it was written. But like all enduring and classical cultural artifacts, it speaks of what is generally human and archetypal. The "people of the book" in some ways represent Everyman and Everywoman.

To use a more technically psychological vocabulary, what the Bible shows is a particular canalization of libido into a highly specific set of human activities, symbols, behavioral patterns, rules and laws, and articles of belief. The pattern created provides a certain defined space for humans to express their physical, emotional, and spiritual desires and aspirations. The Bible is the Constitution and the Bill of Rights, to use the analogy of the United States government, of a religious tradition. It is the rulebook and the reference guide. If in doubt, a person can look it up in the Book and find a precedent. The stories and myths also shape attitude and behavior as much as the specific rules do.

Western people are direct heirs of this tradition, whether we believe in the articles of faith and the pro-positions housed in this sacred text or not. We live within cultures that have formed themselves directly in relation to this Book. The Bible has been, until recently at least, the constant reference point of Western cultures, even if it is no longer an important arbiter in matters of state or taste.

Psychology offers a perspective from which to reflect upon the Bible. The Bible, with its dreams and visions and myths, fairly begs for a psychological interpretation. From this perspective, the Bible is not seen as it would be if one stood within the circle of traditional faith, or if one considered the text as great world literature, or as an important historical document, as or a possible sourcebook of general human wisdom. It is seen rather as a statement of the human psyche. One must understand that this does not invalidate its claims to transcendent truth.

A psychological interpretation of the Bible resembles the psychological interpretation of a dream. In fact, the Bible has many dreamlike qualities. Myths and folk tales, miracles and visions, revelatory dreams and angels and demons all play an important role in the narrative. So as a sort of trope, or methodological premise, I will take the Bible as though it were a dream, even while knowing that this is not literally the case. What this gives me is a way of seeing the Bible and thinking about its meaning. I will take the Bible as I would a dream record, with associations and commentary provided, and the evidence of an ego's work actively structuring the dream experience and knitting it together into a narrative.

The Bible as a whole is of course not literally a dream. In addition to myth, it purports to be history. But because God and the transcendent spirit are such central features of the narrative, even of the seemingly mundane historical portions of it, the unconscious is actively present throughout. It is this feature that must be treated as the most central aspect of the whole discussion. The Bible contains at its very core a mass of material from the unconscious, and psychology provides tools for interpreting this kind of material. The most essential elements of the Bible are clearly visionary, sublime ideas and images that emerge from the dark background of the mind into the light of awareness. This is the purview of depth psychology. A psychological interpretation can make sense of the supernatural elements in the story, which are after all its most important feature.

The Bible is of course made up of contents that are derived from many individuals who are separated by considerable spaces of time. It is not really a single text, the product of one psyche. If we treat it as a dream, therefore, it is as a collective dream series. In addition to the religious visionaries, there are also the historical chroniclers, the scribes who encoded the laws, the poets, and finally, perhaps among the most important, the compilers and editors. As scholarship over the last two centuries has revealed, the Bible shows ample evidence of many hands stitching and many psyches dreaming and having visions. But this does not exclude the possibility of considering the Bible in its wholeness as a single dream, in the sense of taking it as a progressive unfolding revelation of the depths of the collective psyche of this people, the Hebrews and the post-Hebrews (i.e., Christians of the early church). The Bible reflects the processes of the collective unconscious as experienced by this people.

As the dreams and visions of God emerged from the depths and formed a coherent and internally consistent God image, this revelatory material combined with the lived life of this people in history. Synchronistically, a complex of revelations and historical events combined in such a way that inner and outer history joined to produce a *Heilsgeschichte,* a history of salvation or a sacred history. In the Bible, history is as privileged and sacred as are direct revelations of God in visions, dreams, and myth. The symbols of dream and vision are grounded in history, and the history is illuminated and made meaningful by the dreams and visions. The actual creators of the text, the editors, are the conscious egos that pieced together and wove the many elements of the story into the coherence and order that we find in the canonical Bible. For all that, the Bible retains its visionary and symbolic quality to such a degree that history and narrative are more taken up into symbol than the reverse. (This becomes even more evident in the New Testament than in the Old.)

What I would like to claim, then, is that the Bible can be taken as the manifestation of a process in the collective unconscious, which has been filtered through the experience of this particular people, the Hebrew and post-Hebrew peoples, and that throughout the narrative we must sense the presence of the *spiritus rector* that guided the visionary experiences, the history, and the edited presentation. Tradition has called this the Holy Ghost. This *spiritus rector* gives this collective personality its unique stamp.

This does not mean that we are trivializing the Bible. For the depth psychologist, the dream is not a "nothing but" phenomenon. In fact, to give something the status of a dream in analytical psychology is to give it a parallel position of privilege to that granted sacred texts in tradition. As a tradition will look to its sacred texts for revelation – of divine guidance, norms and laws, consolations – so the analytical psychologist will look to the dream for similar depth of vision and understanding. As tradition teaches that the holy scriptures were divinely inspired and that their source of revelation was the holy spirit, so analytical psychology holds that the dream is created by the invisible hand of the Self and that the dream communicates a message from the beyond. So by treating the Bible as a dream we are not reducing it in status. We will take it with utmost seriousness and attempt to find in it meanings that are relevant for ourselves.

Taking the Bible as a dream, then, what kind of dream do we have here? Firstly, it is a long night's dream. The text of this dream was built up over some two thousand years. We must also attend to the truth that there is the dream and then there is the dream text: the one is the primary experience, the other is the edited version. From various studies of dreaming and dream recording, we know that the dream as experienced is not the same as the dream recorded. The former is a good deal more chaotic and in flux than the latter; the latter is much more polished, intact, coherent, and sequential. In transforming a dream into a dream text, the ego does its work: ordering, explaining, censoring, editing, and knitting pieces together. Scholars who have studied the Bible over the past two centuries have uncovered the same identical phenomenon: various versions of similar stories and documents have been edited and re-edited; occasionally portions of the text were censored and repressed; the editors' biases can be discerned in what was chosen and what left out, in the emphases. The two versions of the creation myth in the book of Genesis are a case in point. The value of the work these scholars have done is to assist us in discerning more clearly the original story and the layers of text and redaction. If the unraveling of the text's history has become too much the primary interest of some scholars, this need not deter us from appreciating their detective work. Their work tells us something about the ego's attitudes and defenses. This type of scholarship does not, though, provide an interpretation of the dream's manifest content. That will be left to other interpreters such as ourselves.

So in the Bible we have a long night's dream, stretching over centuries, plus the handiwork of the tradition's ego attitude in the editorial efforts of many scribes and priests.

We also have several versions of the same thing, again as is often found in a night's dreaming. The result of the editorial work is a narrative that is more coherent and organized than the primary experience is, and this coherence can be a block against deeper understanding and experience if we allow our attention to fix itself too much on this aspect. When it comes to interpreting dreams, you're generally better off if you can play somewhat fast and loose with narrative structure. You must reserve the right to jump around in the text, to make odd but telling comparisons of image and figure, to trace subtle underlying motifs that on the surface seem to have little connection. And biblical scholars have done this sort of thing for many generations. For example, the symbol of the tree has been observed to thread its way from the Garden of Eden through the desert where Moses' pole, on which he hoists the serpent, stands for a tree and on to the cross on which Jesus was crucified, which is also identified as a tree. When one is dealing with a long dream, such as this one is, many such resonances of image and motif will leap out at us if we look for them. One of the essential gifts of the talented dream interpreter is to spot these recurrences and to note their repetitions in various contexts and the subtle changes that take place in them as one moves through the text.

Behind this assumed privilege of the dream interpreter is the notion that in the unconscious, time and space are not absolute categories as they seem to be in waking life. If things follow one another in close sequence or proximity, this may say something about their being associated in the un-conscious, but just because they are not so located does not mean that they have no close connection. As we study the Bible we will be moving back and forth in what may seem like an arbitrary manner at times, but at all points we should be able to make the argument of relation by association in the unconscious. After all, this entire dream comes from a single source, culturally speaking.

The dream interpreter has another privilege and holds it very dear, which is not assumed by other sorts of interpreters necessarily. This is the privilege of moving outside the circle of the dream text itself and comparing and contrasting its images with those of other dreams, myths, religions, and archetypal materials. This method of amplification has the function of enriching the symbol under consideration, giving us more of a cognitive handle on it, and thereby providing a depth of insight that would otherwise be unavailable. This is not an exercise in comparative religion for our purposes here, but rather, it is using the resources of comparative religion for determining further layers of meaning in the dream at hand. If references to fairy tales of Grimm's Germany, myths of classical Greece, or beliefs and stories of the American Indian help us to understand the significance of Jacob wrestling with the angel, we will admit these amplifications into our consideration.

The Bible is not only a long night's dream; it is a dream that falls into two parts. There is an "Old Testament" and a "New Testament." This simple fact will give us much material for our interpretation of the biblical text. The fact that the dream is divided into old and new, prior and later, gives this dream a very special quality. In the midst of it, there is a division. It is as though the dreamer woke up for a time, then went back to sleep and dreamt some more. The second part is related intimately to the first, and yet there are enormous differences between them. These differences are important, and how we look upon them is crucial. Simply calling one "old" and the other "new" already sets up tension as though the former has been superseded by the latter. One could as well say, the "first" testament and the "second" testament. But this would of course reverse the nuance, "first" denoting priority and primacy over the "second" and therefore derivative one. These two parts of the dream bring into being a deep cleavage and produce a state of subtle hostility, at least at certain points. But there is also a sense of evolution and development from the former to the latter. During this long night's dreaming, an individuation process is unfolding.

It is not unusual for a dream text to show a sharp break. Things are going along in one way, and then suddenly there is a break and the dream continues on another track, related but still quite other and different. In the biblical case, we assume that it is one dream and that for some reason this dream is broken into two parts. What has happened to cause this break may turn out to be one of the more interesting features of the dream's meaning. In the Bible, there is both continuity and discontinuity between the two parts. In Christian doctrine, it is said that the Old Testament reveals God the Father, the Gospels reveal God the Son, and the history of the church from the day of Pentecost onward reveals God the Holy Spirit. All three are potentially present throughout the text, but their revelation is pegged to a chronological sequence.

There were, of course, strenuous debates in the early church about whether or not to combine the two testaments in the canon. The Gnostics tended to prefer to treat the Old Testament God as a lesser God, if not as a wicked demiurge who should be overthrown and utterly superseded by the benevolent God revealed in the new dispensation. The final decision to combine the two texts in one canon recognized the continuity of the dream's revelation while allowing for the differences to be fully expressed. This attempt to maintain continuity in the tradition can be seen on the one hand as a defense against fragmentation and liminality, which might lead to a sort of borderline state of disintegration and anxiety; it can also be seen, on the other hand, as the product of an individuating personality that is able to bear the tension of uncertainty and the play of the opposites, at least to some extent.

In the following lectures, I cannot attempt an exhaustive interpretation of the dream that is the Bible. I have selected several themes and images for consideration. I believe these are fundamental themes in the dream, but there are also many others. The selection I have made is the following: 1) creation, 2) good and evil, the problem of the Shadow, 3) individuation and the journey of faith, 4) anima images, 5) animus images, 6) election and adoption, and 7) kingship and servanthood. For each of these, several texts will be cited and studied in some detail. Interpreting them, we will bring forward our theoretical tools from analytical psychology to assist with reflecting on the text and coming closer to its meaning.

In the Beginning – Creation

"In the beginning God created the heavens and the earth …" So begins the Bible. Following Jung's advice about dream interpretation, we are bound to notice certain things at the outset of considering an account such as the one before us: time, place, actors (*dramatis personae*), setting, and circumstance. These call for attention initially.

The point of origin – "in the beginning" – refers not only to the chronological beginning of things, but also, and perhaps more importantly, to the logical origin of things; to the *arche* – the fundamental ground plan. This story about beginnings may not be the most ancient and the first dreamed part of the biblical narrative, but this is unimportant. Most likely, as it stands in the text, it is the product of a great deal of editorial refinement and elaboration, and its being placed at the beginning of the Bible was the decision of the compiler and the tradition. It makes logical sense to start at the beginning, even if this is arrived at only after much reflection and thinking. The sense is that we are being presented with a logical mind. The person who is telling us this story is a rational, organized, well-structured sort of personality who puts first things first. Of course, as with all carefully put together presentations, the question of authenticity arises. But is it unusual that, in getting to know someone, the first thing one learns about is the persona, and that the first conversations are coherent and rational?

Certainly this is the case in analysis. The first sessions are the most orderly and coherent. After that, things become more messy and disorderly, but more real as well. Clearly, though, the author(s) of this narrative want us to turn our attention to the origin – the beginning of things – to what is considered most fundamental and archetypal, most formative, that is to say to childhood. We must add that these early passages of the Bible are certainly among the most mythical, and in that sense archetypal, in the entire text. The story about the creation of the world, Adam and Eve in the Garden of Eden, the serpent, the tree of life – these are notable mythical symbolic figures and images and somewhat exceptional in the Bible, which is not overly given to the mythical, the non-historical, and the imaginative. Compared to other creation stories and myths, this one is among the least fantastical and bizarre. If one compares the Genesis account of origins to Hesiod, for example, who tells of the beginning of things in his Theogony, one sees how much more grounded this account is in the natural world and in the realistic, human element. Hesiod describes the origin of creation from Chaos, Gaia, Tartaros, and Eros, and their descendants are a host of fabulous beings who resemble the imaginal characters of an extremely loosely structured, psychotic-like personality. Parthenogenesis, incest, and birth from castrated members produce a host of beings and figures that represent the mental and emotional intrapsychic world more than they do the natural and human/interpersonal one. Hesiod describes the unfolding of imaginal space, whereas Genesis describes the origins and differentiation of a clear, rational, well-ordered, extraverted consciousness. From this beginning, I think we can safely assume that this biblical personality is going to be a "healthy" child and later person, not overly given to brooding and introspection, focused on the outer world of objects, related to the natural environment, clear-headed, perhaps not overly imaginative, and characterized by precision, differentiation, consciousness, and control. From Hesiod, we get the impression of a mind potentially given to psychotic excess, to division and fragmentation, and to an extraordinary range of emotional height and depth. That mental world is "fabulous." From the Bible, we get the impression of a mind in control – of itself, of the drives (animals), and of the potential chaos within the unconscious. If anything, this looks like it might be a psyche given to excessive repression and perhaps to compulsive orderliness and cleanliness.

I once opened a fortune cookie with the wise counsel inside: "Look afar and see the end in the beginning." From this beginning of the Bible, we can see the stage being set for certain predictable problems. The problem of cleanliness vs. pollution and of virtue vs. sin is going to be crucial on physical, moral, emotional, and spiritual levels. Hence, the need for solutions to the problem of sin and uncleanliness is going to become critical. Sacrifice and purification rituals will be needed aplenty, but the discussion of evil in the Bible will be left for the next lecture.

The first character introduced to us in the Bible is also, one will come to realize, the main character throughout the entire text – namely, God. In a way, the Bible is all about God. It is an unfolding revelation of this Person's character and nature. It is not all too often that God is seen directly; mostly He is only spoken about or referred to. But seen or unseen, He is always present in the consciousness or subconsciousness of the text. God is the primary identity given to us through the medium of this long dream that is the Bible, and in the course of it, we can observe Him in various facets and phases of individuation – willing and desiring, rewarding and punishing, suffering and experiencing pleasure. To a great extent, the degree to which you like or don't like the Bible will depend on your feeling about God, on whether or not you like Him. This may, in turn, depend upon your own relationship with your father and on your father complex. For, if this God is anything specific, he is a father. The God who creates heaven and earth is a father God.

It is important to point out that the first character whom we meet in the Bible, i.e., God, cannot be taken as the "dream ego" exactly. Strictly speaking, the dream ego is the character in a dream who says "I." God would be a dream ego if the text read: "In the beginning I created the heavens and the earth ..." and then went on to refer to the God figure in the first person. But as the text stands, there is no "I." No one speaks for the dream ego. There is a reporter, as though the author of the narrative had been present to witness God's act of the creation. But there is also a kind of dream in which no dream ego seems to exist, only an observational awareness that records the events. If you ask the dreamer afterward where he or she is in the dream, they will say: "Nowhere, I was just observing, as though everywhere." In a work of fiction, this is the omniscient author. So we are left with the question: Who had this dream? Who will take responsibility for this report? It can only be affirmed that an observer seems to have been present, recording the events transpiring in consciousness. And, obviously, the only one who could have been present, given the account, is God Himself. So, in that sense, God is the ego of this account. He is the author. This has been the traditional view of the Bible's authorship.

It might be a Jungian temptation to jump to the conclusion that God represents the "self" (not the ego) in the Biblical text, but a number of considerations prevent this facile translation and interpretation. There certainly are self images in the Bible, but God Himself is probably not one of them. God is too much specifically a Father and a hero figure, and the absence of the feminine element in this character militates against His being a self image. Also, He is not inclusive of everything that is, the way a self image by definition is. The "waters" over which His spirit broods and the "earth" that is "without form and void" lie outside of God. God hovers over them, is in charge of them, divides, and subdivides, and adds to them, but they do not come out of Him. "The deep" (*tehom*) is the Hebrew equivalent for the Babylonian Tiamat, a Near Eastern Great Mother Sea Goddess. The spirit of God hovers over Tiamat, the Goddess, and God's act of dividing and subdividing "the deep" is akin to the heroic dismembering of Mother Tiamat by the Babylonian hero, Marduk. In other words, God's act of dividing and separating is the typical act of the hero archetype, the bringer of consciousness, and the necessary precursor of the ego's formation. The ego also divides, separates, discriminates, categorizes, and orders. So it is more that the God image represented at the beginning of the Bible is a proto-ego image, a figure that represents the early and preconscious work of preparation for a developing ego consciousness. Archetypally, this God image is the funda- mental basis upon which the ego will be built, and therefore He represents the possibility for ego consciousness in this personality. When God later creates man and woman in His image, it is simply the further conscious elaboration of this archetypal possibility. The movement from Yahweh to Adam is the psychological passage from hero archetype to human ego.

What we have, therefore, at the beginning of our dream, the Bible, is a presentation of the earliest pre-conscious, archetypal form that the ego personality of this dreamer will assume. Yahweh is the prefigurement of Adam and his descendants. It is true to Jungian developmental understandings that the individual's personality exists wholly "given" in the beginning, but only in *potentia*. As development takes place, this unique personality will unpack itself through a long series of de-integrations and integrations (as Michael Fordham terms it) such that the original archetypal and potential personality gradually becomes humanized and conscious. The archetypes become persons (Mother becomes mother, Father becomes father, etc.) until all that was there in *potentia* is taken up, as it were, into the consciousness of the individual. Thus, if we accept the integrity of the Bible as it stands in Old and New Testaments, as one whole and undivided development narrative, it represents the development of this personality from unconscious potential to manifest realization. The historical Jesus as presented in the synoptic gospels is the endpoint of the development of this prior figure, Yahweh, who is there in the beginning. The story moves from preconscious potential to conscious actualization. When Jesus says, "I and the Father are one," this line of development is affirmed. Jesus is the later realization of the biblical personality, the individuated ego of the unconscious prototype that first presents itself in the opening lines of Genesis. This is what is meant when we say that the Bible represents an individuation process. It is a process that moves from unconscious potential of a unique personality to the manifest realization of that singular individual.

We have the advantage of hindsight, of course. The biblical writers of the pre-Christian era could not see the outcome of the biblical dream as we can from our post-Christian vantage point. We can ask, for instance: How does the figure of God in Genesis, as he is shown to be creating the world and humankind, already show traces of the character that becomes so vividly manifest in Jesus of Nazareth? This kind of question could not be entertained by anyone who had not yet witnessed the outcome of the individuation process. We ask such questions in analysis: How did it happen that the attitudes and hang-ups and emotional patterns I have now first came into being? Can I see my end in my beginning? If I turn out to be a therapist, a caretaker of souls, can I see how I was inclined in that direction already in childhood, taking care of a depressed mother, an alcoholic father, etc. We know how difficult it is to see the outcome of a personality before it has formed and congealed, before the face has set. Until then, there are so many unknowns, so many possible ways and directions development could go. Only in retrospect can we ask: Can I see my pre-individuated face in the photographs from my childhood?

If we take Jesus of Nazareth as the outcome of the personality development depicted in the Bible, can we find traces of His character earlier? And, assuming that the seeds of Jesus' character lie in the figure of Yahweh, can we see how lineaments of Yahweh character are taken up and expressed in Jesus?

As already said, Yahweh is a heroic proto-ego figure. On the first day he omnipotently calls out, "Let there be light," and there is light which he divides from the darkness to make the first complete cycle of day and night. Each subsequent day he shows his complete mastery over the elements. There is no struggle, no resistance, only absolute power. The unruly chaotic forces in Tiamat are utterly subdued; she makes no trouble. This assertion of omnipotence is an expression of a proto-ego that finds its fullest and most realized expression in the heroic figure of Jesus of Nazareth. Jesus is a realized hero in the egoic sense of the word: not omnipotent but fully conscious; utterly masterful in the handling and choosing of his own fate and destiny; and completely independent and successfully separated from his mother, who also, like Tiamat, gives him no grief in his freedom of choice and action. Reading ahead from Genesis to the synoptic gospels, we can readily see how Jesus represents the individuated ego that presents itself in a mythic, archetypal form in Genesis as the Creator God, Yahweh.

Reading the other way, backwards to the beginning, we can also see features of Jesus in Yahweh, though much less defined because of the unconscious nature of this figure. When John says, "In the beginning was the word, and word was with God and the Word was God," he is affirming the notion that Jesus is the culmination of the Yahweh personality and that the seeds of the former were there in the beginning with the latter. The emphasis on "word" again implies consciousness. As Jesus represents new consciousness, or consciousness realized within the domain of ego awareness, so Yahweh represented the earliest possibility for consciousness. Jesus is a teacher of spiritual truths and laws; Yahweh was a lawmaker and a lawgiver. Jesus is single-minded and dedicated to his sense of purpose and his mission; Yahweh was similarly dedicated – to his mission in the world in and through the chosen people. Jesus is a judge who expresses a mercy and empathy; Yahweh was a judge who gives his people many second chances. But perhaps most fundamental of all from a psychological structural point of view is the feature in this personality that relates to the feminine and to evil. Jesus separates from his mother early and decisively ("I have no mother") and lives his life outside of marriage or significant relationship with a woman. Yahweh was shown creating the world by himself, without a mate or spouse. The feminine is held at arm's length, or repressed.

And evil is "other" – the serpent, Satan, Judas. This personality that comes into being through individuation in the biblical text exemplifies the heroic patriarchal masculine ego, whose highest values are rationality, order, clarity, consistency, control of emotion and of bodily instinct. An extreme commitment to the heroic achievement of spiritual purity and mastery over the natural world, including the ego's self-preservation defenses, characterizes this personality.

If we point out the limitations and defined structures of this personality that comes into being in the biblical text, we do so without criticism or desire that it should be other than it is. We accept it as it is, and attempt to relate to it in its particularity and concreteness. In some respects, we may not like it, but we must also recognize that all of us have our limitations, particularly so as we individuate. To individuate means to become an individual. To criticize the biblical personality for not being other than it is would be like criticizing an oak tree for not being a maple. We can expect of an oak only that it will be a good oak, that it will show individuality and the features that are particular and wonderful to it. So it is in the case of the biblical personality. We can imagine other life scripts for Jesus of Nazareth, but if he had been other than he was, he would not have been himself and he would not have fulfilled the development of the biblical dream. Kazentzakis imagined Jesus' "last temptation," thinking through how it would have been if Jesus had left his preferences and sense of mission and had lived another kind of life: wedded, becoming a father of children and thereby integrating the maternal and feminine aspects into his personality structures. But this is a "temptation" to betray one's calling to the path of authentic individuation and to live another life. Yahweh has no spouse; his "children" are not natural ones, they are adopted in a sense, i.e., spiritual not physical children; He does not embody secularity but remains true to His spiritual essence, heroically renouncing the flesh and its pleasures. In the terms given by our dream, Jesus represents the fulfillment of the archetypal possibility shown originally by Yahweh in the very first moments of creation and throughout the text up to the point of Jesus' birth.

The dream figure, Yahweh, is also presented as Creator. In this respect, He is the archetype that imprints itself on a personality as that personality assumes and forms its structures. Yahweh creates himself through his creative work in nature and human culture. The first explicit instance of this action of the Yahweh figure regarding human beings is the creation of Adam and Eve. The story of paradise and the drama that unfolds in it are a second creation story. This one is much less cosmic and more human that the first one. We can relate to it more easily. It is on the earth and reminds us of experiences of our own childhood. The figure of God retreats somewhat into the background as the new characters emerge and the story unfolds. We are moving from an image of the preconscious basis of the individuating ego in the Yahweh of Genesis to an image of preconscious childhood, of the ego in the warmth of the mother world. Paradise is an image of the positive mother, and the condition for staying in this state of paradisal unconsciousness is to remain unconscious.

In Adam we have the earliest form of the human ego, perhaps even intrauterine. Yahweh's imprint is on him, but Yahweh's knowledge and power are far from his understanding. He is the germ of ego consciousness. In Adam, the Biblical dream depicts its own earliest self-awareness of being sentient, contained in the mother, innocent of danger, without want or need. Adam does not ask for Eve; Yahweh sees his need for a companion and fulfills it. Eve, coming from Adam's side, represents an anima, the first differentiation of the feminine from the masculine side of self-awareness and identification. Eve is other and vaguely associated with the animal instincts, i.e., closer to the unconscious and therefore a potential mediatrix to the unconscious, to its potential rewards and dangers.

One thing we become aware of early on in the Biblical text is the careful way in which this personality presents images of the feminine. We will delve into this later in more detail, but already we can see a certain wariness that leads us to ask about defenses. One would expect, quite naturally, that an image of the Great Mother would belong to the account of creation and childhood, particularly the latter, since our first experience of the world is the female body, the mother. Greek Gaia is the source of Ouranos, for example, and then the matrix of many other creatures, culminating in humankind. Our earliest childhood is spent in the psychological circle of the mother and in her physical presence. Our transitional objects, which allow us to separate gradually from her, represent the mother and comfort us because they stand in for her when we are apart.

This being the case in nature, we have to ask what is going on when the presence of the mother is so carefully denied and occluded. The defense against the mother to this extent would imply an overly strong attachment to her and the concomitant need to deny her importance. We do know that this biblical dream took place within the cultural context of great Mother religions, and that much of the strenuous emphasis on the supremacy of the father and the making taboo of Mother Goddess emblems (the "pig" for example, symbol of fertility and the plentiful breast) had to do with the Hebrews setting themselves off from the cultural environs. Their "chosenness" set them apart from the Mother worshippers, in addition to identifying them with the Father. So there is in the suppression of the Mother and of the feminine generally, a masculine protest against Her power. To say that the feminine comes out of the masculine – Eve from Adam – is almost humorous in its obvious preposterousness. As a dream image, it is compensatory to the overpowering influence of the Great Mother. There is a sort of violent separation of infantile masculine ego from the smothering arms of the mother.

Despite the protest and the over-compensation, though, images of the feminine and the mother continue to creep into the picture. Tehom, "the face of the deep," for example; the image of the Garden of Eden as a containing maternal image; the tree and its fruit; Eve herself, who becomes the mother of the human race; but all of these are rendered in this portrait as being under the firm control of the heroic masculine, the Father, a Creator God figure. The mother has been mastered, and the power of the feminine over the masculine ego has been placed in severe check. God designates Adam the master of Eve. Yet, the drama that unfolds in the garden demonstrates that the feminine wiles have not been completely subdued and defeated. What is left to them is to lead the immature masculine ego into folly. The female has become seductive. She remains a danger because of her connection to nature, to the instincts, and to a kind of contrarian spirit of willfulness. This is also, of course, a depiction of the individuating influence of the anima, even in the earliest phases of masculine development.

In Jungian theory, it is argued that the anima stands opposed to the persona. The persona is adaptive to the outer world – the world of social conventions and customs. The anima, on the other hand, is renegade, unconventional, and individuating. In this respect, she is quite different from the mother, who fosters persona adaptation. The anima is the bit of sneaky personality that a man holds in reserve when he makes public promises. And this leads him, typically, into disobedience, as it does Adam. Just as typically, he wants to deny responsibility: "she made me do it." Because the anima is not ego-syntonic in the early phases of development, she operates outside of the area of ego responsibility, and the ego has no control over her comings and goings. In the drama between Yahweh and Adam, we see the dynamic of a parent-child separation/individuation process at work. Adam disobeys and is removed from the warm nest in Paradise. Having to leave the garden, never to return, is an event of ego alienation from the maternal unconscious as well as from the protection of the parents in the state of childish innocence. Adam is forced to leave the nest, and the pain and regret he faces is a bit harsh, but normal for the development of a masculine ego that must realize its capacity for endurance, suffering, hardship, and limitation. Adam represents the ego individuating out of the mother, leaving the containment of childhood, and venturing into the world of work, taxes, and death. We see this theme of heroic separation and individuation repeated many times in the biblical text: Abraham leaving home; Moses leading the Hebrews out of Egypt; Jesus carrying his cross to Calvary. The knowledge of good and evil received as a result of eating of the fruit of the tree turns into the awareness of reality as it is experienced by the limited human ego when it becomes conscious. This knowledge comes about through the act of disobedience, which is a crucial feature of our story, for the obedience vs. disobedience struggle is one of the central themes of the biblical narrative. It is one of the most crucial questions of the individuation process, and it leads to the discussion of sin, guilt, and evil that will form the discussion of the next lecture.

The Shadow

At its outset, the Bible depicts its chief figure, God, as being in complete control: He dominates *tehom* (Tiamat), He calls out for light and there is light. He divides and subdivides things and brings order into the world laid out before Him until one can see a cosmos – a coherent image – inclusive of plants, animals, and humans. God is pictured as both ordering and creating, i.e., making things to fill in the picture until it is complete, and He can rest. The image we are presented with in these opening passages is of a solitary, ordering, controlling, creating archetype.

As we proceed with our psychological reading of the Bible, we will consider all of the images and events contained in it in relation to this central figure and to some extent as representative, or expressive, of Him. He is the "I am" in the biblical dream, and all figures and aspects of the dream are parts of Him. This is His story. It will become apparent that this figure is quite complex and more interesting, from the psychological point of view, than one would at first suspect. We learn about Him from what He does, we get to know Him by what He creates, and we learn about Him directly and indirectly as the story unfolds.

Yahweh appears throughout the text of the Bible as a figure who demands obedience from the humans he created in His own image and endowed with an amount of freedom to choose for themselves. He is possessive and He is jealous. The humans are not robots; they have free will and autonomy. This creates the problem. They are like the psychic complexes in a person's unconscious, unruly and with a will of their own. Obedience to God's will, His commandments, and His plan for the humans on earth is the cardinal virtue espoused in all the books of the Bible. God is a psyche struggling for control of Himself and all His parts. The conflicts around obedience and disobedience lie at the heart of the drama that is the Bible. It is an agon whose outcome is always in question until the very end of time when there will be a decisive battle and scores will be settled, sadly without resolution. There is a part of Him that remains disobedient to His will to the end, that cannot be contained or integrated and must be brutally suppressed. The Bible is not a comedy, it is a tragedy; it's more like "Hamlet" than like "All's Well That Ends Well."

After the initial creation, the story continues and includes the human level with Adam and Eve placed in the Garden of Eden. God gives them instructions: they may enjoy the Garden and eat of the fruit of the trees, only not the fruit of the trees of life and the knowledge of good and evil. Thus, the theme of obedience and its opposite, disobedience, emerges right at the beginning. This theme runs on throughout the rest of the Bible: obedience to God's calling and will on the part of Abraham, obedience to the Commandments given to Moses, Job being tested for faithfulness and obedience, the prophets' calls to obedience, Jesus' perfect obedience ("Not my will but thine be done"). Why is obedience to God's will such an important matter?

Then there is Satan. A powerful and independent counterforce to the dominant Yahweh and a convincing shadow figure, Satan is disobedience personified.[1] Satan and Jesus represent the opposites: disobedience vs. obedience. While it is not particularly surprising from a human point of view that a divisive and controlling Father would insist on absolute obedience to His will on the part of His children, and thus create violent enmity between them, it is still necessary to reflect further on this paramount biblical virtue in order to grasp its deeper psychological meaning and purpose.

As an aside, when Freud introduced the concept of the superego into his theory of the three-part mental structure – consisting of the id, ego, superego – Jung commented humorously that he was smuggling Yahweh into his psychology. In Freud's understanding, the superego relates to the ego as a strict parent: admonishing, condemning, criticizing, and castigating, but also demanding certain ideals of the ego. From Jung's point of view, Freud was speaking of an archetype in his doctrine of the superego, and Jung could see the similarity between it and the biblical Yahweh. Yahweh acts like a superego figure in the way that He seeks obedience to His rules and norms, as well as to His will rather than to other competing tendencies like pleasure in the fleshpots of Egypt. He also serves as a superego figure when He is able to use His fury to punish offenders by killing, as He does in the great Flood, for example, or in the story of the golden calf. Yahweh's fury against his people is legendary, and the "fear of the Lord" is a frequently repeated admonition.

---

[1] See Rivkah Kluger's chapter "Satan as Independent Demon," in *Satan in the Old Testament* (Evanston, IL: Northwestern University Press, 1967), 149-162.

THE BIBLE AS DREAM

In his late work, *Answer to Job*, Jung comments on the
difference between the Hebrew Yahweh and the Greek Zeus.
The latter, he says, is much more detached from and in-
different to the human realm; he is distant, only occasionally
interested in what is going on in the sub-Olympian world.
Yahweh, on the other hand, is passionately engaged in what
is happening among the chosen people; for Him, it matters
immensely what the people are doing. He chooses his people
and makes incredible demands of them, and then He watches
them with a hawk's eye. He is what we would see in human
terms as a terribly intrusive parent, hovering over everything
His children are doing and constantly criticizing them. Jung
writes: "Zeus too could throw thunderbolts about, but only
at hopelessly disorderly individuals. Against mankind as a
whole he had no objections – but then they did not interest
him all that much. Yahweh, however, could get inordinately
excited about man as a species and men as individuals if they
did not behave as He desired or expected, without ever
considering that in his omnipotence He could easily have
created something better than these 'bad earthenware
pots.'"[2] The point here is that Yahweh did care to an extreme
degree, as though this were the most important project in
the universe, and what He cared most about was obedience.
He is trying to organize them, and He uses rewards and
punishments to do so. Moreover, there is going to be a final
reckoning – a Day of Judgment. This is something all humans
have to look forward to.

Yahweh's concern about human beings to this extent
gives the Bible its particular quality and tone: God really

---

[2] C.G. Jung, *Answer to Job*, in *Coll. Wks.* 11 (Princeton, NJ: Princeton
University Press, 1969) par. 568.

cares about what we do and even think! God regards it as supremely important that the human individual, and also humanity as a whole, follow His directives and instructions and keep His Commandments. The "chosen people" are supposed to show the way and be the example of this attitude of devotion and obedience. Yahweh's attitude looks like that of a highly anxious person, afraid that something terrible will happen if he follows his instinctual inclinations instead of the book of rules, but it is essential to recognize that Yahweh's concern is not only, or even primarily, for the welfare of humans. In fact, it may be true that people will generally live better and more productive lives if they are obedient to the Commandments, but it is even more important that they obey for another reason: By obeying His will, they will become like Him. They will realize the pattern of *imago Dei*. They will incarnate Him on earth. This is the powerful insistence of an archetype to realize itself in a precise way and enter human consciousness in its fullness. If consciousness departs from the archetypal pattern by even a little bit, the image will not be true to the maker, and the pattern will not be realized.

Yahweh's insistence on obedience is the insistence of a Creator who wants the object He is making to turn out exactly as He wants it, as it exists in His mind, and even more that it reflects Him precisely. Yahweh wants the human figure to be shaped exactly to His will, in His image, for it is only in this way that He will become embodied accurately and fully in His creation. They have free will because He has free will, which is not easy to manage. He is trying to get fully born and realized. So what we see in this biblical dream is the story of an archetype trying to become born and realized in consciousness, to become fully taken up within the ego awareness of the mind. Disobedience is a departure from the desired image. In a way, disobedience is easier, while obedience is a very demanding psychological project.

Yahweh's urgent demand for obedience creates the central dynamic of the dream, which is the constant tension and interplay between obedience and disobedience. This, in turn, creates the distinctions between purity and pollution, innocence and guilt, and honor and shame. The insistence on obedience immediately implies the possibility of disobedience, and with disobedience comes disorder, shame, guilt, and the need to hide one's terrible knowledge gained thereby. In the biblical dream, one of the first and most crucial events is, in fact, the act of disobedience. It is this act that sets the whole ensuing drama into motion, culminating in the crucifixion of Jesus to redeem the sins of the world.

The distinction between good and evil is a basic discrimination of human consciousness. Its origins lie in early childhood. It is a discrimination that begins as good/bad in terms of objects – good breast/bad breast, good mother/bad mother, good friend/bad friend (enemy). Then it also quickly gets applied to parts of the self – good thoughts/bad thoughts, etc. This is a normal part of becoming conscious and of ego development, and it comes about with or without the assistance of a harsh or too observant parent. The experience of shame, however, can be more or less exaggerated and become pivotal in further development only if strongly emphasized or reinforced by parental authority. Everyone experiences shame, and everyone experiences its effect of isolating its victims from others. Shame drives us into a corner by ourselves, outside the warmth of community, often into intolerable pain and isolation. The experience of Adam and Eve is the experience of shame. They become aware of themselves, of their nakedness, and in acquiring this forbidden knowledge they suffer the pain of shame.

It makes good sense that a God who wants voluntary obedience would need to create situations of temptation, otherwise there would be no opportunity to demonstrate the necessary virtue. In the Garden of Eden, He creates the perfect matrix for His children, Adam and Eve, and places into it two objects that are forbidden: a tree of life and a tree of knowledge. It is noteworthy in our story that Eve and Adam are tempted to taste of the tree of knowledge (of good and evil) rather than of the tree of life. Apparently, know-ledge is both forbidden and especially desirable in this personality. This is a personality that is going to have a strong desire to know, perhaps even stronger than the desire to live. Melaine Klein spoke of the "epistemophilic instinct" and speculated that it was this intense interest on the part of the infant that led to explorations of the mother's body and to the knowledge of good and bad breasts. The infant's desire to know is a sign of its potential for mental growth. If this were not inherent in an infant, it would have to be implanted. The infant, in order to become a mature human being, is going to have to learn a tremendous amount of cultural material. The human species is wired such that knowledge is not a "given" from our instinctual make-up; we survive and thrive because we have the drive and the ability to learn, to gain knowledge.

It is not knowledge in general that the Lord forbids. He may approve of certain kinds of knowledge: the names of things such as the plants and animals in the garden, but he prohibits knowledge of good and evil.

This would be totally contradictory to my thesis that Yahweh is an archetype that wants to be incarnated in human form to also say that He did not want humankind to know good from evil. For it is precisely, as the serpent says, by knowing good from evil that Adam and Eve will become like God. So, we would have to conclude that God put the tree in the garden knowing full well that Adam and Eve would disobey him and would eat of it, because he wanted them to do so. But then what about the punishment? What about the shame? Well, God knew this too. As the dream presents itself, God knows everything, is in complete control of everything, and is totally masterful. While it seems that he loses control so easily to a couple of innocents, surely He could not have been that simple. We have to see it as a set-up; God intended it. He planted the trees there. He did the one thing necessary to ensure the tree's fruit would be eaten by forbidding it to Adam and Eve. He sent the serpent to tempt Eve, knowing that she would fall for the bait. He intended that they disobey Him and feel shame, and thereby come to know good from evil. That was precisely the lesson. They had to learn the difference between good and evil in order to become like Him. From this, we must assume that God also knew the difference between good and evil in a similar way. Moral intelligence is especially valued in this story.

Remember, He is recreating a consciousness on the human level that He has on the archetypal level. The sense of guilt and shame – guilt for committing a crime of disobedience, and shame for knowing something forbidden – must characterize Yahweh's consciousness also. We know from the rest of the story that expiation for guilt becomes a major theme in this personality: how to get rid of it, how to sacrifice, how to rid oneself of sin, and how to keep from falling into sin. There is a tremendous shadow problem here.

The people who come into being through the election of Yahweh ("the chosen people") are known historically for observance and the Law. Their mission as a collective is to incarnate obedience to the high standard of the Law. The major founding figure of this people is Moses, the lawgiver. Moses is not responsible for creating the law. He channels it from Yahweh. The Ten Commandments are only the basic laws, however. There are many more minute derivative laws that eventually cover most of the contingencies of life in the society established according to the Commandments. In the end, there would be little room left for doubt about what was right and proper conduct in reference to most any facet of human life: family, sexual relations, marriage, personal hygiene and cleanliness, proper and improper foods and how to prepare them, public policy, and management of contracts. This personality became extremely, perhaps excessively, legalistic. Laws were multiplied to cover everything. It begins to resemble a compulsive personality with ritualistic observances for this and that, in the desperate hope of achieving and maintaining a state of purity and cleanliness. Somehow, though, the stains of pollution and shame are extremely difficult to wipe away and keep away. Sin is an act, which produces guilt, but it is also a condition, which requires expiation, sacrifice, purification rituals, and elaborate ceremonies. One result of this highly differentiated knowledge of sin is a high level of consciousness, of a particular sort. Another result could be a serious problem with self-esteem. It is as though from the beginning of the biblical dream onwards, this personality is dealing with the issue of shame and guilt, as though some primordial sin had been committed. This resulted in patterns of cleaning, vigilance, and ritualistic activities. In psychological shorthand, we would say this person had an undealt with shadow problem, and that all the attempts at self-purification were ineffective because the true source of the problem was not being addressed. One would have to get to the underlying issue, to the original crime, and address that rather than the details of everyday life, which are merely symptomatic. Freud would trace this back to primal murder of the Father, the original sin.

The figure that best represents the shadow in the biblical dream is Satan, or the Devil. It is generally conceded that the Devil makes his first appearance in the figure of the serpent who tempts Eve in the garden. Because Eve listens to his seductive words – "your eyes will be opened and you will be like gods, knowing good and evil" – and allows her curiosity and "epistemophilic instinct" to override Yahweh's words of instruction and His command, she commits the unforgivable act of disobedience. The resulting sense of shame and guilt manages to implant itself irrevocably in the consciousness of the first humans and parents of mankind. This experience and its aftermath, the terrible consequences of banishment from Eden and the vulnerability to death, mark the consciousness of the biblical personality from this moment forward. Later elaborations in theology would speak of "original sin," a condition into which all are born and which implacably pursues human consciousness from early years to late.

From a normal human point of view, this development of consciousness in which good can be discriminated from bad would seem to be a good thing – an outcome to be desired. Its absence would not bode well for the individual or for the community. Yet, the price paid for this consciousness is the realization that one is not all good and innocent.

It is a consciousness that backfires, in a certain way. At first, good and evil are "out there," but rather quickly, and in the case of Adam and Eve instantaneously, the same discrimination is applied to the self. From here on and forever after, consciousness is burdened with the question of good and evil, inner and outer. Am I good enough? Do I measure up to the standards set for me? And the doubting thought that I am not good enough, that I do not do what is right and that I leave undone that which should be done, haunts consciousness. Sometimes we think that "conscience" represents the voice of God, but who is to say that it is not the voice of the Adversary – the doubting thought within God himself?

Another important appearance of Satan in the Old Testament occurs in the opening lines of Job. God enters into a dialogue with Satan, who has been going up and down on earth and observing things. Satan is an aspect of God's consciousness – a "roving eye." God points out his faithful servant Job to Satan as an example of the obedient man he so much craves and adores. Satan raises the question, would Job remain faithful and obedient if he were not so successful and prosperous? Of course he is upright – it pays! But test him; take away his property and his family, humiliate him, and then you will see his true colors. In this instance, God Himself falls into temptation and acts on Satan's advice. Satan represents God's doubting thought, his own skeptical attitude. As Iago represents Othello's jealous thinking, which undermines his ego position and confidence in the words of his beloved Desdemona, so Satan represents Yahweh's doubts about his seemingly obedient servant, Job.

From this image of the heavenly court as depicted in the Book of Job, I think we can safely say that the archetype that is trying to incarnate itself in this individuation process depicted in the Bible is of two minds. At the outset of the Bible, in the opening chapter of Genesis, Yahweh seems single-minded and masterful in his clarity of execution, but it quickly develops that He is more complex, and one of these complexities is the presence of this tempting, doubting aspect of his personality: Satan. As the dream continues, both Yahweh and Satan undergo further elaborations at the level of ego consciousness, and ego consciousness becomes burdened with the same duality as is evident in the archetype. The result is a strenuous but hopeless struggle to be obedient and faithful to a high calling and vision of what should be, and continual failures and attempts to get back on the path. No sooner does one get back on the path, though, than temptation and doubt reappear and again lure the ego elsewhere. Shame, guilt, self-doubt, and a keen consciousness of right and wrong, lawful and unlawful, clean and unclean are the result. As St. Paul says, the law leads to consciousness of sin. He also cries out: "who will deliver us from this burden?"

The desire for final and ultimate deliverance from the burden of the law and its consequences for consciousness, namely sin, comes to culmination in the New Testament. Here, the sharp opposition between obedience and disobedience and good and evil comes to a climactic expression in the figures of Jesus and Satan, or Christ and anti-Christ. At this point in the dream, the development of tension between good and evil within this personality reaches a crescendo. Satan becomes more sharply delineated as a result of the contrast with Christ, and he also takes on the features of deeper evil. The New Testament represents a supreme crisis in this personality. Never before have the issues been so starkly drawn between good and evil, life and death, and obedience and sin. As we observe the dream unfolding, we get a sense of a critical extreme in the tensions inherent in this personality. The forces of good and evil are building toward a climax, and this climax occurs dramatically in the story of Jesus and its aftermath.

Jesus meets Satan on a number of occasions and resists his sly temptations to disobedience and separation from the will of the Father. In this sense, he is a point of contrast with Adam and Eve, but also with Yahweh as portrayed in Job and certainly with the chosen people who are continually falling into sin and away from righteousness and obedience. Jesus dialogues with Satan, engages in active imagination with his shadow, obedience confronting disobedience, submission to the Father's will standing up against rebellion and self-assertion – and sharply, repeatedly, and decisively Jesus rejects the insinuating thoughts of Satan. What began as a somewhat subtle and minor-looking cleavage in the archetype back in Genesis, then showed itself in a more elaborate way in Job as Yahweh and his doubting thought now reaches the stage of fierce opposition that threatens total splitting apart into opposing and absolute power centers. No longer is Satan a part of the heavenly court; he is clearly the enemy. The opposition between ego and shadow has reached a dramatic crisis. This is the climax of the dream.

One way of looking at the story of Jesus is to see it as the attempt on the part of this personality to incarnate fully into ego consciousness. In so doing, however, it splits into two parts, as unconscious contents typically do as they enter consciousness. In other words, the archetype disintegrates. One piece of it becomes ego-integrated in the figure of Jesus, while the other piece remains outside of consciousness, and therefore remains more mythical (does not become an historical individual) and works its way into history indirectly through the action of a "mob." Mobs and groups in dreams generally represent the activity of an unconscious content in the background; it has not yet formed into one coherent personality. It is as though a magnet is operating beneath a surface of metal filings: the filings move around but the cause of their movement is invisible. In the story of Jesus, we have a figure who embodies Yahweh partially and takes on the conflict in this archetype by battling the other part in the form of an invisible Satan. Satan is the shadow that is not integrated into consciousness. The conflict between these two parts is so severe that their division into the opposites of good and evil causes the enmity between them to become absolute – to the death.

Who wins? There are several possible answers: Satan wins because evil overcomes good and destroys Jesus; Jesus wins because he rose from the dead and ultimately overcame Satan and threw him into the fiery furnace forever and ever; or neither wins because the personality is torn apart and ends in permanent neurosis. A fourth answer may prove more satisfying, but for that one we need to read the dream text closely, and discriminate between at least two strands that are presented in the New Testament: the synoptic gospels and Pauline epistles on the one side, and the Johannine works on the other. These, it seems to me, offer somewhat differing resolutions. The major question we face is this: does the biblical dream represent a personality that ultimately falls into irreconcilable inner conflict and breaks down, or does it represent a personality that develops to the point of crisis and then reintegrates on another level after the crisis has been survived?

Faith and Individuation

There are a number of great stories in the Bible, and they are strung together to form a coherent narrative that tells of the formation of a people, Israel, and its internal and external struggles and development. On one level, the story can be read as a family history, but the significant difference from most generational family stories is that the entire narrative is about how this family relates through time to its singular ancestor spirit, Yahweh. So in another sense, and this is the one we have been pursuing in our reflections, the story is really about Yahweh and only secondarily about history. History is, as in a dream, the background of the archetypal dynamic of unfolding and incarnation. Yahweh expresses Himself in and through history, and in the form of this people He attempts to incarnate Himself. In psychological terminology, the Bible represents the psyche as a portion of it attempts to move from one side – the "unconscious" – to the other, to ego-consciousness.

In earlier lectures, we studied the beginnings of this process as described in the Book of Genesis. There, in the story of Adam and Eve in the Garden of Eden, we see the first evidence of egohood. It seems innate to egohood that it should be "disobedient," that is, make up its own mind despite instructions to the contrary. The ego's assertion against the parent creator, which is supported by the side of the parent God that is His own split-off rebelliousness, initiates the separation from the womb of paradise and leads the way to the entry into awareness of life as struggle, limitation, and alienation. The ego has become separated from the original self, and the experience of shame and guilt and anxiety comes with this second birth.

In the previous lecture, we tracked the problem of shadow splitting and differentiation within this personality at both the archetypal and personal levels: Yahweh's shadow problem is reflected on earth, and the human problem with shadow splitting and integration both results in and mirrors this same phenomenon at the archetypal level. What comes into being is a personality made up of a keen awareness of the difference between good and evil, and a constant struggle between obedience and disobedience. Sin comes into the world, and this means the sense of uncleanliness and pollution at the most primitive level and of moral and spiritual failures – "missing the mark" – at higher levels. Sin is alienating, and it further removes the ego from the archetypal parent that is wanting to incarnate itself precisely in ego consciousness. The story of the relation between this alienated and disobedient ego longing all the while for restitution and closeness to the father archetype is the story of the Bible: man sins, is restored, sins again, sacrifices and is restored, sins again and falls away, is called back and is restored, sins again and is punished, repents and is restored, sins again and is forced to wander in the wilderness or in exile, is restored, sins again, and on and on.

Then there are the giants of faith who leave behind every security and follow the command of God: Abraham is the prime example. He leaves his home at the command of Yahweh and even brings his son, Isaac, to the point of sacrifice out of obedience to God. There is also Moses who, though reluctantly at first, leads the children of Israel out of bondage in Egypt to the promised land. Moses is a partially successful embodiment of Yahweh: a hero, a lawgiver, and a father of his people. Between Abraham and Moses we have a pretty accurate portrait of the archetypal figure behind this story: a father who is courageous and decisive, and a heroic leader who defies the odds of captivity by Pharaoh's armies to lead the people out of bondage into freedom. As Rivkah Kluger points out in her essay, "The Chosen People,"[3] Egypt came to represent the Great Mother, and the leave-taking from her is therefore an individuation/separation story: ambivalence, looking backward, and insistence on an absolute separation from her. The people of Israel leaving Egypt repeats on the historical level what took place archetypally at the beginning of Genesis: creation through separation, first of the elements in the cosmos and then of the fledgling human ego from the womb of paradise.

Exodus tells the story of the creation of the chosen people: Moses discovers God at the burning bush on Mount Sinai, receives his instructions, heroically leads the people out of the motherland, and assists them in forging an identity in the wilderness that centers on their relation to Yahweh. In developmental terms, this would be equivalent to identity formation, and one could compare it to adolescence and identity formation. In the wilderness and under the leadership of Moses – himself a representative of Yahweh who

---

[3] Rivkah Kluger, "The Idea of the Chosen People in the Old Testament: A Contribution to the Symbolism of Individuation," in *Psyche and Bible* (New York: Spring Publications, 1974), 3-43.

speaks to Yahweh face to face – the Hebrew people make
their basic life decision and find their destiny:

> And Moses summoned all Israel and said to them:
> "You have seen all that the Lord did before your
> eyes in the land of Egypt…You stand this day all of
> you before the Lord your God, the heads of your
> tribes, your elders, and your officers, all the men
> of Israel, you little ones, your wives, and the
> sojourner who is in your camp, both he who hews
> your wood and he who draws your water, that you
> may enter into the sworn covenant of the Lord
> your God, which the Lord your God makes with
> you this day; that he may establish you this day as
> his people, and that he may be your God, as he
> promised you, and as he swore to your fathers, to
> Abraham, to Isaac, and to Jacob… See, I have set
> before you this day life and good, death and evil. If
> you obey the commandments of the Lord your
> God, which I command you this day, by loving the
> Lord your God, by walking in his ways, and by
> keeping his commandments and his statutes and his
> ordinances, then you shall live and multiply, and
> the Lord your God will bless you in the land which
> you are entering to take possession of it. But if your
> heart turns away, and you will not hear, but are
> drawn away to worship other gods and serve them,
> I declare to you this day, that you shall perish; you
> shall not live long in the land which you are going
> over the Jordan to enter and possess. I call heaven
> and earth to witness against you this day, that I have
> set before you life and death, blessing and curse;

therefore choose life, that you and your descendants may live, loving the Lord your God, obeying his voice, and cleaving to him; for that means life to you and length of days, that you may dwell in the land which the Lord swore to your fathers, to Abraham, to Isaac, and to Jacob, to give them."[4] (Deut. 29:2, 10-13; 30:15-20)

Here, the children of Israel are presented with the fundamental choice of identity: they are to cleave to this one God and only to Him; they are to obey Him and no other; they are to reject all other archetypal possibilities. This is the Covenant – a sort of legal contract between God and His people – which seals their identity and bonds them permanently to Him. Once Israel has its law and its identity, Moses can die and return to the archetypal realm of the Fathers.

It was Freud's (perhaps darkly ironic and in a sense "disobedient" or subversive) suggestion that Moses was not a Hebrew but an Egyptian prince who remained loyal to Pharaoh Akhenaten's revolutionary monotheism when regimes changed and went back to the earlier polytheistic religion in Egypt.[5] Freud argued that it was the Egyptian Prince, Moses, and not Yahweh, who "chose" the Hebrews, led them out of his homeland, and introduced them to the high (and according to Freud, unbearable) ethical standards of monotheism. As far as individuation goes, it must also be recognized that in order to secure a definite identity, and for

---

[4] Deuteronomy 29:2, 10-13; 30:15-20.
[5] Sigmund Freud, "Moses Was an Egyptian," in *Moses and Monotheism* (London: Hogarth Press, 1939), 11-28.

one singular archetype to manifest itself clearly in ego-consciousness, other archetypes must be (often violently) excluded, and this entails struggle and sacrifice. Yahweh puts the issue starkly in terms of life and death: come with me and live, or depart from me and die. A psychological price to be paid for this kind of firmness in ego identity is inevitably guilt: one has slain the Great Mother, the source of all the archetypal possibilities. A slightly different way of putting it is that one has exchanged omnipotence for uniqueness (David Gutmann[6]), which is the essential act for overcoming the "puer aetenus" complex (eternal adolescence and consequent lack of choice and identity), which involves killing the mother of all possibilities and making a definite commitment to a single path.

What we have in the biblical narrative by the time Moses dies, then, is a solidly established ego personality of masculine patriarchal cast based on an uncompromising repression of the mother-unconscious, a horizontal split and an identification with the heroic father archetype. Ego boundaries are clear and firm in one respect: identity is established by the covenant. In another sense, however, ego boundaries are not necessarily clear, considering that there is an identification with an archetype which can, and does, lead to inflation. The inflation manifests itself as this people hurls itself across the Jordan and into the promised land: it feels itself called by God to capture this land, and it has the feeling of entitlement and specialness characteristic of archetypal identification and resultant inflation. Out of this inflated sense of self, it believes that its own will and self-

---

[6] This is a brilliant phrase that David Gutmann used in his classes on midlife and adult development at Northwestern University.

interest are identical with the will of God. For the purposes of combat and securing the desired territory, this attitude is extremely effective. It induces acts of incredible courage and daring, as well as acts of horrible cruelty: the Hebrews take no prisoners but utterly obliterate the indigenous population. The Christian Europeans entering into the promised land of America came with this same sense of superiority over the native peoples. The attitude of "we are here by divine right and blessing" is an ego inflation based on identification with an archetype. The usual price for inflation is, ultimately, disastrous because of overreach. Reality-testing becomes insufficient, and relationships with one's environment are distorted. The environment, whether natural or social, eventually strikes back and humiliates the inflated ego. But for the stretch of life that we can identify today as early adulthood, from the point of identity formation up until midlife, this kind of inflated attitude is characteristic, to some extent even necessary for establishing the personality in this world, and useful for securing a safe space for the creation and rearing of a family.

A person needs this kind of inflation for the energy it brings and the illusory self-confidence that can override the many obstacles thrown in the way. The individual typically has to push itself into an already crowded world and make a space, and then secure it in the best way possible. In order to do this, certain scruples must be overridden. The overly sensitive young man is unable to create this kind of niche for himself, and therefore remains dependent on his parents. If the Israelites had lacked confidence, had been ambivalent, had been squeamish about killing off the indigenous populations and setting up their own cities, they would have failed to establish themselves. And to do this, they needed the identification with the divine will. It is one thing to kill because the ego wants something (this is psychopathy); it is another to kill because God commanded it (this is heroism, and we decorate such soldiers after victory in war). God gives the ultimate imprimatur for violating His own laws for the sake of claiming a space in the world. Individuation, we could equally say, often demands violation of mores and conventions that otherwise are considered sacred: obedience to parents, fidelity in relationships, and honoring contracts and bargains. But the permission for breaking these laws must come from a source beyond the ego's own ability to permit or deny the discharge of impulse. As Jesus said of the man who was working in his fields on the Sabbath in an apocryphal story: "Blessed is he who knows what he is doing; otherwise he is cursed." Transcending the ethical imperative is an act to undertake with fear and trembling, and certainly with great consciousness.

Eventually, as the narrative continues, the children of Israel do manage to take the promised land and to become masters of this territory. They build a capital, Jerusalem, and in it a great temple to their God, Yahweh. Politically they have evolved from a tribe led by chieftains to leadership by so-called Judges, and finally they arrive to kingship. The emergence of a dominant center as symbolized by the king (Saul, David, Solomon) and the gradual integration and centralization of power in the figure of the political leader, the religious priesthood, and the temple, all of which are located in Jerusalem, is consolidation of the ego. All of this represents ego consolidation and integration under the authority of the dominant archetype informing this identity from the unconscious, Yahweh. All of this history is refinement on the themes stated in the early days, in the creative period. Nothing significantly new is added as far as personality development is concerned.

And then comes crisis, fragmentation, loss, destruction: the kingdom of Israel is overrun by the enemy forces of Babylon and the people are taken away into captivity. After a number of years in Babylon, they are allowed to return to their homeland, but never again are things the same as they were. There are always occupying forces – Babylonians, Persians, Egyptians, Greeks, Romans – and foreign rulers, culminating in the destruction of the Temple and the dispersion of the Jews out of the land in and after 70 C.E. This is the historical backdrop, and our interest is not so much in this as in how the biblical personality was developing in and through it. The disaster and fragmentation that occurred to the nation naturally produced a great internal spiritual crisis and upheaval. Questions arose: had faith been broken, trust betrayed? Had Yahweh deserted his people? Or was this punishment for sin? Prophets called the people to obedience and expanded the understanding of the law. They heard the voice of the Lord calling His people to obedience and promising rewards and good things to them if they returned to faith. Through all of this upheaval and crisis, this personality, while tested, did not break nor give up its fundamental identity as a special people chosen by Yahweh, but its self-understanding changed. Gone is the sense of entitlement, and what appears now is more the concept of service: this people is special, but they are meant to be priests to the nations. It becomes a less self-serving personality and more one dedicated to service in a broadened sense.

Its identity also shifts significantly from warrior and king and ruler (the heroic identity of the earlier period) to a more mature, modified, less inflated sense of service and servanthood. And yet the dream of the homeland, of the promised land, of a land with boundaries secured and a temple in the midst of it, continued to haunt the imagination of this people. They longed for the old days and yearned for a return to the days of youthful vigor. Out of a combination of longing for an earthly kingdom, the old kingdom, and a sense of higher calling and service to all of mankind came the notion, the image, and the dream of the Messiah. The promise and expectation of the Messiah was born of this crisis period. The Messiah would somehow deliver the people, restore the land, protect the nation against its enemies, and set up the kingdom of God on earth. Few understood exactly who or what the Messiah would be. He was the anointed one, the new king, a hero, or God Himself in human form. The biblical personality was in a state of liminality, ungrounded, fragmented, and therefore also open to a new revelation of the archetype divine.

Let me review the thesis briefly: it is that an archetype named Yahweh comes to a place of prominence ("constellates," as we say) in the collective unconscious and begins to create an ego identity, which will become an incarnation of it. It does this at a price, however; the price is repression of other archetypes, and ultimately of the Great Mother, and a split in the psyche. Ego identity in the form of the human figures in our narrative takes shape around this archetypal core and replicates its structures within the realm of consciousness. The ego, built upon and identified in this way with the archetype of hero-father, Yahweh, consolidates itself and establishes a position for itself in the world. This will be a family with a name and an ongoing living connection to its mythical source. Having attained its goal, a process of disintegration gradually begins which culminates in near collapse. One can see this in the squabbles of the sons of the great kings and in their competition and rivalry that diminishes and weakens the kingdom. A sort of midlife crisis now takes place: confusion, loss of some identifications (the land, the kingdom), breakdown of ego boundaries, mourning, grief, and loss; then comes wandering and severe liminality and early attempts at reintegration, which fail. In this state of liminality at midlife there emerges the beginning of another possibility for identity, based more on service and mission than on heroic conquest. The image for it shifts from king to servant; generativity, service to the others and to the future generations; a broadened sense of responsibility and meaning; and a deeper understanding of the self, including feminine elements. It is during this liminal period that the prophets, such as Isaiah, Jeremiah, and Ezekiel proclaim their message. As well, the wisdom literature – books such as Job, Proverbs, and Ecclesiastes – are composed at this time. Arguably the greatest and most profound literature in the Hebrew Bible is composed at this time, and it is undeniably on a par with the elevated thought and poetic magnificence of sacred texts from others of the great religions. This is a deeply religious period, not a period of conquest, heroics, and rulership. It is a period of reflection, of deepening understanding of the human condition, and of suffering, and it is a time for exploration into the depths of the self beyond what has been know consciously heretofore.

The ego here opens more than usual to the unconscious. It is in a shattered state of deintegration, suffering, and turmoil, and therefore also especially close to the archetypal background of the psyche. Out of this background there emerges the image of the Messiah. I will consider the image of the Messiah as a new archetypal image proceeding out of the collective unconscious, a new archetype coming forth to take its place in ego consciousness beside that of the hero father figure. The biblical text affirms the unity of these two figures, the father and the son, but ultimately it also demonstrates that the son is not simply a renewal of the father sent to restore the status quo ante. The archetypal process underlying the biblical text is not one of death and rebirth, which is a cyclic process characteristic of persons and cultures identified with the Great Mother – the great cycle of nature that repeats itself each year. Rather, it is a pattern of birth, growth, death, and transformation, a pattern that is not repetitious but evolutionary.

There were, of course, those who expected the Messiah to be a renewal figure who would restore the old kingdom, but they were disappointed. The Messiah who appears comes preaching that his kingdom is not of this world, but of heaven. And it is in this message of the kingdom of heaven and his further gift, the Holy Spirit, that one comes to understand how it is that Jesus of Nazareth is critical for the further individuation of this personality.

In dreams, the birth of a child, particularly of a magical child, augers an appearance of the self. The child represents a new future, based upon a new archetypal possibility. Another archetype is penetrating into consciousness and will eventually demand integration. Jesus is born into an already old and crowded psyche. There is no room for him in the inn, so he enters through the doorway of a lowly manger, a sort of little trapdoor in consciousness through which he can climb. The story of his birth and first months follows the pattern of the birth of the hero: born under unfavorable circumstances, threatened with death, barely surviving. This was also the story of Moses' birth. But the psyche is preparing for his arrival. The dream tells of visitations by angels and other extraordinary phenomena, such as a star in the heavens leads the wise men to Bethlehem. Dreams instruct the principle players in the naming of John and Jesus. And, most significant of all, Jesus has no human father: he is begotten of Mary and the Holy Spirit, something that is utterly out of place in the biblical narrative which tends to be realistic about such matters. This unusual and mythical parentage sets him aside and designates him as an archetypal symbol.

As I pointed out in an earlier lecture, Jesus of Nazareth is the closest approximation to the fully obedient son of God there is or could be. In this sense, he is an incarnation of the archetype of Yahweh. In other respects, he is very different from Yahweh as that God is portrayed in the earlier narrative. For one thing, Jesus is not a father figure. He never does embody this aspect of the Yahweh archetype. Yahweh is so much a father that this contrast is highly significant. Jesus is a son, so as a divine figure he represents something different from the father God who begets him. In one sense, Jesus incarnates Yahweh, in that he is obedient to the Father's will even unto death, but in another sense, he incarnates something quite different. It is a seeming paradox in our dream that the father appears before the son, though of course in naturalistic terms this is the way it must be. In developmental terms, however, the son precedes the father. Every man is a son before he is a father. Before Jesus, the people of Israel – the chosen people – were the children of God, but they were his by adoption. Jesus is his by birth. The biblical context into which he is born is one that had already formed itself through a long preceding history and consolidated its identity around

67

the father archetype. It is this identity that Jesus challenges, as a son might challenge a father in order to become himself. But Jesus does not do this. He comes not to destroy the law but to fulfill it, as he claims. Nevertheless, he does confront the father religion of the Israelite nation, and in this manner, challenges the psychological identity and structures that had been established in the previous centuries. In Jesus' actions and in his relations with the religious elders – the Pharisees, the priests, and the scribes – he faces off against exclusive dedication to the law. The law represents the concretization of this people's identity and of its identification with Yahweh. Jesus challenges this. One among many instances being when he says, "man is not made for the law, but the law for man." Jesus heals the sick on the Sabbath, forgives sins, eats with the untouchable tax collectors and prostitutes, and generally breaks down the restrictive boundaries of the law at every turn, but without himself becoming a criminal or a sinner. As he puts it, no one would pour new wine into an old wine container, so what he is about is destroying the old container and fashioning a new one in order for the new wine to be held in it.

Psychologically speaking, this means breaking down the old identifications, character structure, and habits of thought and behavior, and preparing the ground for new structures. Jesus furthers the process of deintegration that had been at work in this ego identity for some time. As he breaks down the old structures, he is constantly pointing to a new structure, which he calls the kingdom of heaven. This will be the new container for the new wine; the new structure of ego consciousness that will hold a new expression of the archetypal self. Jesus overrides the real and legalistic imperatives with a message that they are not enough and that the old personality must be transformed through destructuring (death) in order to reconstellate around a new center of identity.

Many parables are told about the kingdom of heaven – stories that hint at the new psychic constellation that is coming into being. Stories are told and images presented when a content is still too unconscious to be formulated in more precise conscious terms. Theology follows story, dream, and image. The stories and myths hint at something that is still mysterious – still "out there" in the beyond somewhere, not yet integrated sufficiently into consciousness to become fully understandable. Many of Jesus' stories tell of the great value of the kingdom of heaven and of how one must sell all in order to enter it. This means one must give up all earlier identifications in order to become new or to enter into the new constellation. There is a new birth – "you must be born anew," as he tells the Pharisee Nicodemus[7] – and one must become as a little child and therefore without the accumulation of complexes and baggage carried by an older personality. The message of Jesus is "die and be reborn a new person." From the viewpoint of the self, this is a story of the destruction of one consolidation of ego-consciousness and the creation of another which embodies the self in a fuller way.

In a sense, the Yahweh archetype self-destructs: it sacrifices itself, in order for the new constellation of itself to be born into ego-consciousness. There is the puzzling mystery of Jesus' death and of the Father's demand that he be sacrificed. I must admit, I have puzzled about this necessity a great deal. Was it really necessary for Jesus to die,

---

[7] John 3:7.

and if so, why? It seems so cruel. The usual explanation is that this was necessary for the forgiveness of sin. Jesus is an innocent lamb that is sacrificed to remove the sins of others. But from the viewpoint of the biblical narrative itself, taken as a dream of individuation, it would have to be said that Jesus was sacrificed so that something new, namely the Kingdom of Heaven and the Holy Spirit, could be born into consciousness, and that the sacrifice really was Yahweh sacrificing himself in order to make way for this transformation. So long as Yahweh continued to claim dominance, there seemed to be no way out of the repetition of sin and sacrifice. The underlying problem, namely Yahweh's guilt for killing the Great Mother, never was dealt with, and could not be dealt with unless he was willing to sacrifice himself in order to make room for something else to enter ego-consciousness. So Yahweh actually did what he at first asked Abraham to do and then prevented by replacing the sacrificial son with a ram. Yahweh did indeed sacrifice his only son, who represented an extension of Himself into the future. If a father in a patriarchal culture loses his only son, his line is dead, and this is what we see in this biblical dream: a father sacrificing his only son and thereby creating a vacuum into which other contents can come and form a new identity. The death of Jesus left this sort of vacuum.

The disciples are portrayed as shocked and confused. The Messiah has disappointed them, too. They are left with nothing but dreams of glory, all in the past. And then something happens. They see the risen Christ, they are reoriented, and finally they receive the gift of the Holy Spirit. Instead of a human leader, king, teacher, or magician, they now have only a spirit. And what a spirit it is. It creates some kind of mystic states in them, and they can speak in strange tongues. They can heal the sick. They are empowered to preach the gospel of the Kingdom of Heaven and to spread the word. They are on fire. In short, they are filled with a new archetype and its extraordinary energy, and they are quite puzzled about how to control it. It is a mysterious thing, the Holy Spirit, but it directs them. They realize they cannot control it. And most astonishing of all, it takes them beyond the boundaries of the children of Israel, the chosen people.

This is a spirit that crosses boundaries of nation, tribe, sexual distinction: Jews and Gentiles, men and women, slave and free, it seems to know no human distinctions of social class or caste. It is a universal spirit, and it forces them to become universal men. The spirit leads them on long journeys throughout the known world; it teaches them that they can eat unclean meat; it claims that the law may be important for some on the persona level but it does not matter ultimately. In the Holy Spirit, we can see the release in this personality of the transcendent function: the *spiritus rector*, or the guiding spirit of the self that is not under ego control but rather controls the ego and gives it purpose and a mission in life.

Of the three persons in the Holy Trinity, as this was later conceived in theology, it is the Holy Spirit who most nearly represents and speaks for the self. It is a reconciling, peace-bringing spirit; it is sometimes imaged as feminine, some-times masculine, sometimes neither; it is a connecting, linking spirit, the spirit of love; it transcends any sort of ego boundaries or identifications and leads into freedom from the law; it reconciles the opposites and joins consciousness with the unconscious. As a symbol for a new kind of attitude, it comes as close as we can conceive to an attitude in ego-consciousness that embodies the self maximally. Insofar as this personality, as presented to us in the Biblical narrative, achieved this – a new container for this new wine – it achieved full individuation.

Anima Images

In dealing with the Bible as a dream and taking up our interpretive position as though we were looking at the contents of a dream dreamt over several centuries by a multitude of individuals, we must keep reminding ourselves that the dream is a reflection of unconscious processes at work in the collective unconscious. This keeps us from falling into the concretistic fallacy, which would have us take the story at face value and repeat it to ourselves as history. On the one hand, this helps us with the elements in the Bible that are clearly mythical and metaphorical, elements like the story of creation and the Garden of Eden and the Virgin birth of Jesus. To be consistent, however, we must also treat the elements that are explicitly historical as dream elements, reading history for symbolic meanings as they emerge from the unconscious. This is not so different from treating the Bible as the story of the unfolding of God's plan in history, since that viewpoint, too, interprets history as the concrete expression of an invisible hand at work in the background. In a sense, then, treating the Bible as a psychological text — viewing the story as we would a dream — brings us closer to the Bible's self-understanding as the revelation of God's plan in and through history than a purely secular and historical reading of the Bible, for example.

From our vantage point as psychological interpreters, we have discerned that the Bible is about a personality whose central, guiding, and controlling inner figure is Yahweh. Yahweh represents the archetypal dominant upon which this story centers. In the course of the story, Yahweh reveals much about His nature, His personality, His traits, and His characteristics. He becomes a clearly defined personality, and in this sense is not so different from the gods of other pantheons, such as Zeus, Wotan, etc. But one great and impressive difference between the Yahwistic mythologem and that of the others one thinks of is the exclusivity of His presence in the heavenly realms. He is the lord and master of His kingdom, and others who may exist in and around Him – servants such as the angels or other types of minions in His court – are there only by His consent.

Because there is an absence of other deities in His court, one is not so immediately impressed by the absence of any sort of female deity. If there were a group of other gods besides Yahweh, then it would be more apparent what a large gap the absence of feminine deities leaves. But as it is, one is less inclined to note the absence of the Great Goddess. The few references to a feminine companion of Yahweh – the Sophia of the Wisdom literature – do not go very far to redress this absence, but they do remind the reader of precisely that absence, and they are important passages for alerting us to a movement in the dreamer's unconscious that is seeking to compensate for the picture's one-sidedness.

If we look on the "ground," however, we see quite another picture. At the level of the story that represents itself as history in this world of time and space, the feminine is represented in a great variety of ways. And it is these figures that we must look to in order to investigate the place and the role of the anima in the biblical dream.

Before proceeding to look at the anima images that are available in the text of the biblical dream, we should pause to note some notions about Jungian dream interpretation that pertain to the subject of the anima. In his early formulation of the concept of the anima, which is detailed in the "Definitions" chapter of *Psychological Types* under the heading of "soul" and "soul image," Jung defines the anima as an autonomous complex, or "personality," that constitutes the person's attitude toward the unconscious. This psychic structure, which is innate *qua* structure, not as specific content however, stands in a complimentary relation to the "persona," which constitutes the person's habitual attitude toward the outer world. Typically, in a man's personality, the persona is made up of aspects of the personality that fit in with personal and cultural definitions of "manhood," i.e., forms of the masculine. The anima, by contrast, is made up of aspects that remain unconscious and take the configuration of a female figure. Moreover, the man typically identifies with the persona and suppresses, represses, or otherwise fails to include and integrate so-called feminine elements into his conscious personality, and these, clustering together (around an archetypal core) and making up the anima, are experienced not directly within but as "outside" in projection. The projection carrier, then, represents the anima attitude of which the man is unconscious. If he wants to know what his anima looks like, he should consult the image of the women he tends to fall in love with. Invariably, as Jung states it, this image of the anima will be complimentary to his persona attitude.

Complimentary does not necessarily mean exactly in opposition to, but usually there is a tension – a significant difference in values, personality traits, and psychic orientation. Thinking types tend to fall in love with feeling types, extroverts with introverts, heroes with victims, etc. In dreams, these figures are represented, again typically, by same sex and other sex figures. The same sex figures will indicate something about the persona, or shadow element of the persona, to be distinguished from the anima, while the opposite sex figures will indicate anima constellations. Jung observed that it was particularly the same sex (in this case, male) figures who are idealized and held up as models of accomplishment and esteem that represent the persona values with the person who is striving to identify himself. The anima and the shadow typically have elements in common, since both are excluded from the persona and represent the rejected and repressed aspects of the personality.

For a woman's psychology, the set-up is exactly the same, only one speaks of the animus, rather than of the anima, as the attitude facing toward the unconscious. Structurally, however, there is no essential difference between anima and animus. Moreover, the content of both is highly variable and dependent on cultural factors.

As we look at the biblical dream using this theoretical framework for our interpretation, we will identify the ideal masculine figures as persona images and the feminine figures as anima images. These, we will find, do have a sort of complementary relation to one another, and tensions between them are not infrequent. The psyche dreaming this dream repeatedly tries to shore up the persona. It finds the anima interfering, distracting, or downright contrary, but does seem to slowly and gradually move from repression toward integration of the anima. This is an early generalization and may need to be revised as we go along.

The first appearance of the anima in the text, as it is presented to us by the redactors of this dream, comes in the first chapters of Genesis, bearing the name Eve. We need to consider this appearance of the anima with special care, since it is the initial dream, if you will, in the series, and therefore states much about what is to come. The text gives us two accounts of the creation of humankind. The first states: "So God created man in his own image, in the image of God he created him; male and female he created them."[8] From this, we get the fundamental notion of homology between God and man: we are in the same image. The profundity of this casual remark is underscored by the image of syzygy: the "image" that mirrors God's own image is a male/female image, a pair that, using Jung's interpretive notions, represents a person/anima relation. The accent in the Bible is so strongly on masculine identity that the obvious interpretive stance is to regard it as the dream of an essentially masculine personality – of a man. In our next lecture, we will consider it as a dream of a still deeper sort, in which the dreamer is essentially feminine in character. But for now, at the level we are considering the text, we can assume that the masculine archetype, Yahweh, is creating an identity that is going to mirror Him, an essentially masculine personality with some feminine (anima) features in the background.

The text makes the point of masculine priority rhetorically: "…in the image of God he created him; male and female he created them." Clearly, the accent falls on "him"; this is a male dominated personality, and the major

---

[8] Genesis 1:27.

77

conscious identification is going to be with the masculine element. The second creation story elaborates this point in mythological form. First God creates Adam, and then, when He observes that it is not good for man to be without a partner, He puts him to sleep and creates Eve from one of his ribs. Again, the text states that the anima is derivative from and dependent upon the constellation of the male persona. Functionally, the anima compliments the persona. The story that ensues tells of the tension between these features of this personality.

Adam, the representative of the persona, obedient to the commands of external authority, does not face the temptation of the serpent directly. The serpent, representative of the deeper layers of the unconscious, approaches him via the anima. As Jung says, the anima faces to the unconscious and is subject to pressures from this source, whereas the persona faces outward and is subject to pressures from the external environment. In this drama, Yahweh is culture, and the serpent is nature. And here we see the first conflict between the proclivities of the anima and those of the persona. The anima is open to the voice of nature's temptations. The serpent was a sacred animal of the Great Goddess and may favor a competing religion of goddess worship. At any rate, the image of God, the Adam/Eve figure, is subject to inner tensions – the one part tending one way and the other quite differently. Eve's vulnerability to the seduction of the serpent makes her, in turn, a seductress of Adam.

At this point in the story, Adam is not yet strongly enough established in his identity to resist the wiles of the anima, and so the tension is resolved in her favor. The anima proves stronger in this personality than the persona at this stage of early development. From this, one could very well understand Yahweh's anxiety about this creation of His: it is unstable. Mankind's consciousness cannot stand up to the tension of the opposite built into its system, and it is for the purpose of strengthening the masculine persona side of this personality that much of the remainder of the biblical dream is directed. Adam, who represents the ego-consciousness constellation in this psyche, needs to be strengthened to the point where he will not succumb to the serpent or to the anima. Many of the biblical heroes show us this virtue: they are impervious to the blandishments of the anima, of nature, of Baal worship, of the mother, and of the Goddess religions around them. The tragic heroes, those with fatal flaws, like Samson, succumb to the anima figures who tempt them: Delilah stands in line with Eve as a powerful and over-whelming anima for a fragile and vulnerable masculine ego-persona structure. Other heroes are able to resist her – Joseph rejects the blandishments of Potiphar's wife, and Elisha defeats Jezebel and her prophets of Baal. Others, like King David, succumb but then manage to right themselves in the end. The decisive struggle does not take place, however, until Jesus faces temptation down resolutely.

The resolution of the story of Adam and Eve and the Garden of Eden comes when Yahweh confronts them with their regression: they have not lived up to his command-ments and intervention must therefore be instituted. Yahweh's intervention should not be seen only as punish-ment, although the text indicates this intent primarily. There is also a theological significance to the fall from grace and the dismissal from paradise. After all, this sets the human pair on the road to development and greater consciousness, which are also important biblical themes. The intervention of Yahweh also takes place in order to rectify a power arrangement that he had not created quite so explicitly before: he places Adam firmly in authority over Eve. The masculine element is clearly to rule the feminine and the feminine to submit to the masculine. This intervention is delivered in order to strengthen the masculine persona against the inherently more powerful feminine element and to guard against future regressions. This is a delicate work of adjustment, for God clearly does not want to totally alienate the pair from one another. After all, they need each other in order to fully represent the God image.

In creating female along with male, Yahweh was acknowledging His own feminine aspect. But her absence in the heavenly court also indicates a strong repression of her, a splitting off of the Great Goddess that had set Father Yahweh up as chief of the heavenly realm. This has also had the effect of isolating Him and cutting Him off from His anima element, which would connect Him to deeper levels of the collective unconscious and the self. In creating Adam and Eve as His image, He is trying to redress the imbalance.

At first this does not work, because Adam is not strong enough. God will have to try again and again before he succeeds in finding one strong enough to be able to afford a genuine relationship with the anima, a relationship that is not based on defensiveness or domination. But this is a long ways down the road of history.

If Eve sets the tone for the anima image in the biblical dream, she does not exhaust all the possibilities. There are other kinds of feminine figures that appear from time to time in the dream. Perhaps a crude line could be drawn down the middle of all the anima representations in the Bible that would place the Eve types – the seductresses; the head-turning, wayward tending, nature-oriented types – on one side, and the loyal, faithful daughter and mother types on the other. Cast in the first role are figures like Eve, Noah's daughters, Potiphar's wife, Delilah, Jezebel, Bathsheba, the harlot whom Hosea married, the New Testament woman caught in adultery, Mary Magdalene. Sometimes Israel itself is referred to as being this kind of a woman. Her basic character is out of tune with the ideal of the Yahwistic persona type: she is a temptress, she leads astray, and she runs after other gods. She represents the temptations of nature and the flesh. In her darkest colors, she is the witch: one of the devouring, angry, monstrous figures that are more hinted at than represented in the text. When the anima is constellated as this subversive figure, we must assume that there is too strong an identification with the persona, or, more likely, that the persona needs to be further strengthened by distancing itself from the powers of the anima. When the anima shows a strongly negative face in dreams, it usually indicates the danger of regression, of identifying too closely with anima elements to the detriment of the masculine identity. As we know from the outset, this biblical personality tends to be unstable and vulnerable to the anima and must therefore seek safety in distance and repression.

On the other side of the ledger, there are feminine figures who play an essentially positive, supportive role in relation to the masculine persona figures. There may be a slight degree of tension between the men and these women in their lives, but the tensions are subsumed under cooperative arrangements. The women support rather than seduce the Yahwistic heroes. In this column are figures such as Abraham's wife, Sarah; Rachel and Rebekah, the tribal mothers; Hannah, Samuel's mother, who prepares her son

THE BIBLE AS DREAM

for service in the temple; Ruth, the dutiful daughter-in-law; and Esther, the savior of her people. There is the "fiery woman," Deborah, and the fierce woman she praises, Jael, who kills the enemy general, Sisera, by driving a tent peg through his temple. Hear the fierce words of Deborah as she sings of Jael's militant heroism:

> "Most blessed of women be Jael,
>   the wife of Heber the Kenite,
>   of tent-dwelling women most blessed.
> He asked water and she gave him milk,
> And brought him curds in a lordly bowl.
> She put her hand to the tent peg
>   And her right hand to the workmen's mallet
> She struck Sisera a blow,
>   She crushed his head,
>   She shattered and pierced his temple.
> He sank, he fell,
>   He lay still at her feet;
> At her feet he sank, he fell;
>   Where he sank, there he fell dead."[9]

Here we have the triumphant cry of the fierce warrior anima who supports the work of the Lord as He directs His chosen people in the conquest and securing of the promised land. Anima figures like this appear when the masculine element is weak and ineffectual and needs strengthening. Deborah functioned as a judge during a time of oppression and captivity, when the Canaanites had fallen under the rulership of the tyrant Sisera and his army. She and Jael

---

[9] Judges 5:24-27.

represent the compensation from the unconscious during a time of persona crisis, when the masculine persona is suffering grievous humiliation. Her fierce militant attitude and caustic irony as she scorns the thought of Sisera's mother waiting for him to return home with spoils and captive women for his troops underlines the elevated rhetoric of the poetry.

> "Out of the window she peered,
>   the mother of Sisera gazed through the lattice:
> 'Why is his chariot so long in coming?
>   Why tarry the hoof beats of his chariots?'
> Her wisest ladies make answer,
>   Nay, she gives answer to herself,
> 'Are they not finding and dividing the spoil?—
>   A maiden or two for every man;
> Spoil of dyed stuffs for Sisera,
>   Spoil of dyed stuffs embroidered,
> Two pieces of dyed work embroidered for my neck as spoil?'
>
> So perish all thine enemies, O Lord!
>   But thy friends be like the sun as he rises in his might."[10]

There is a thrill of war and a shout of victory. Deborah is a father's daughter, like Athene or Brunhilde, a type of anima attitude that has given itself over totally to the service of the masculine heroics. In a man's psychology, this type of anima insures against despair and inner collapse in the face of catastrophe and extreme adversity. More than a comforter, she is an active ally, picking up the fallen sword and carrying

---

[10] Judges 5:28-31.

on the battle fervor when his spirit would fail. These women do not seduce, lead astray, and tempt the person toward the soft lineaments of pleasure and regression; they support the opposite movement toward a buildup of the heroic persona. These are the daughters of the Lord.

The anima takes another form later when, in the 3rd and 2nd centuries B.C.E. the figure of wisdom, Sophia, makes her appearance. Sophia is the closest one comes in the biblical text to a goddess figure: she is transcendent and belongs in the heavenly court as the companion of God, and thus has the attributes of a divine goddess. Sophia can be compared to Isis and Demeter, the great goddesses of the same period belonging to Greek and Egyptian mystery religions. Though there are tensions in Sophia, by and large she is seen as the helpful companion of Yahweh, helping him work out his plan with Israel in and through history. Contrasted to her is the figure of Folly, an anima figure who captures the qualities associated with the other kind of woman. The writer of the Proverbs counsels:

> "Say to wisdom, 'You are my sister,'
>   and call insight your intimate friend;
> to preserve you from the loose woman,
>   from the adventuress with her smooth words...
>
> And lo, a woman meets him,
>   dressed as a harlot, wily of heart.
> She is loud and wayward,
>   her feet do not stay at home;
> now in the street, now in the market,
>   and at every corner she lies in wait.
> She seizes him and kisses him,
>   and with impudent face she says to him:

'I had to offer sacrifices,
  and today I have paid my vows;
so now I have come out to meet you,
  to seek you eagerly, and I have found you.
I have decked my couch with coverings,
  colored spreads of Egyptian linen;
I have perfumed my bed with myrrh,
  aloes, and cinnamon.
Come, let us take our fill of love till morning;
  let us delight ourselves with love.
For my husband is not at home;
  he has gone on a long journey;
he took a bag of money with him;
  at full moon he will come home.'"[11] (Proverbs 7:4-20)

Folly is a further expression of the anima we find in the figures of Eve, Potiphar's wife, and Delilah. We might call this the Aphrodite aspect of the anima – an unfaithful love goddess. By contrast, consider Wisdom:

"I, wisdom, dwell in prudence,
  and I find knowledge and discretion.
The fear of the Lord is hatred of evil.
Pride and arrogance and the way of evil
  and perverted speech I hate.
I have counsel and sound wisdom,
  I have insight, I have strength.
By me kings reign,
  and ruler decree what is just;
by me princes rule, and nobles govern the earth."[12]

---

[11] Proverbs 7:4-5; 10-20.
[12] Proverbs 8:12-16.

What we see in this division of anima figures is the resistance of the unconscious to come along totally with Yahweh's project of creating a patriarchal personality. In part, the anima will support the Yahwistic masculine dominant, as we see in figures like Deborah and Wisdom, but in part, the anima resists this development and calls Yahweh's people to abandonment of this project, as well as to sensuality, to regression, and to the fleshpots of Egypt.

What we see in the anima images of the Bible, then, is a tension between the Yahwistic imperative for this biblical personality to constellate a conscious attitude that conforms to the Yahweh dominant archetype, which is supported in part by the anima, or else it would have no chance of success whatsoever, but also resisted. This can be stated as the tension between the spirit and the flesh, between Law and physical desire, between a masculine ethical culture with its values of rank and authority and a more impulse-oriented, pleasure-driven, sensual, feminine culture. The New Testament will state this as the struggle between the Old Adam and the New Man: the Old Adam representing the weaker constellation who gave into Eve's temptation and regressed, the New Man a stronger constellation able to resist.

The mother of Jesus, Mary, is the counterpart to Eve. Eve is a kind of unstable version of the anima that Mary more purely and stably represents, just as Adam is an unstable Jesus. Adam and Eve represent but a rather unstably constellated attitude that reaches fulfillment or completion in Jesus and Mary. As Jesus is the perfect son of the Father, so Mary is his perfect daughter. She is an anima who completely and without reservation supports the will of the father, not in the militant strident fashion of a Deborah, but in the receptive and humble attitude of perfect servant. In

Mary we see the anima as the pure and undistorting function that facilitates the smooth passage between archetype and ego-consciousness, or between Yahweh and human history/ Israel. This function had been performed earlier in the biblical dream by prophets who heard the will of God in a still, small voice and passed it on to the people. Mary is the prophet's attentive ear who receives the divine will and passes it on through herself. And Jesus is the voice of God. Mary's attitude of receptivity and service to the Father is perfectly expressed in the famous lines of the Magnificat:

"My soul magnifies the Lord,
and my spirit rejoices in God my Savior,
for he has regarded the low estate of his handmaiden.
For behold, henceforth all generations will call me blessed;
For he who is mighty has done great things for me,
and holy is his name.
And his mercy is on those who fear him
from generation to generation.
He has shown strength with his arm,
he has scattered the proud in the imagination of their hearts,
he has put down the mighty from their thrones,
and exalted those of low degree;
he has filled the hungry with good things,
and the rich he has sent empty away.
He has helped his servant Israel,
in remembrance of his mercy,
as he spoke to our fathers,
to Abraham and to his posterity forever."[13]

<hr>

[13] Luke 1:46-55.

Mary is unlike Eve in that she is conscious of a history that refers back to Father Abraham, and she is totally dedicated to the service of Yahweh. Mary is a refinement of the side of the anima that has supported Yahweh all along in his efforts to form and shape a people in his image. Any trace of inclination toward sensuality, the voice of the serpent, sexuality, material possessions and finery, or any other features so vividly displayed by Folly, is totally absent from this anima image.

The doctrine of the virgin birth of Jesus, which is such a remarkable feature of the story of his origin, has sometimes been misunderstood as a rationalization of the shadow of the young girl, Mary, who got herself pregnant or was raped by a Roman soldier and then had to come up with a good story to sanitize herself. This sort of projection into the dream text on the part of would-be interpreters simply muddies the waters with their own shadow material. The story of the virgin birth is not a cover-up but rather a statement made necessary by the later life and meaning of Jesus. The virgin birth did not make Jesus divine; rather, the divinity of Jesus made the virgin birth necessary. Virginity means purity and the absence of the other side of the anima, which pulls toward materiality and the sensual. Mary is the anima of spiritual purity.

As dream interpreters we must ask: What is going on in this personality that this kind of dream is necessary? Dreams compensate for the condition of ego-consciousness and promote its development and individuation toward ultimate wholeness, and in this case, toward a full embodiment of the archetype represented by Yahweh and more, including the denied and split off aspects of the self that Yahweh has suppressed. In this instance, the dream of the virgin anima, the spiritual father, and the perfectly obedient son is a powerful compensatory effort from the unconscious for an ego-consciousness that is in dire danger of losing its spiritual orientation altogether and collapsing into regression and gross materialism. The psyche is powerfully shoring up the spiritual side. This was the necessary compensation for the danger facing the people of Israel during these difficult times: Israel was occupied by Rome and its extremely contrary values, struggling for some measure of independence and religious autonomy and freedom, more and more obsessed with the fine points and details of the law as it applied to the material aspects of everyday life, drawn toward political uprisings and insurrectionary movements that would drain the spiritual life of the people completely into secular concerns. The historical epoch into which the young woman Mary and her son Jesus were born did indeed call for a new centering of the ancient identity first proposed by Yahweh to the Hebrew nomads some two thousand years earlier. This personality was in danger of spiritual and moral collapse, hence the dream of the virgin birth, the spiritual anima, and her gift to the people Israel.

The rejection of this gift by Israel simply underscores the conflict between ego-consciousness and the unconscious that typified this time in Israel's history. Mary and Jesus introduce into the biblical dream the strongest possible image of Yahwistic spiritual ideals. Mary is the anima of spiritual idealism as her son is its animus. This idealism, of course, intensifies the conflict between the opposites inherent in this psyche to the point of climax in the book of Revelation, where the dark and uncooperative side of the anima is represented by "the great harlot," commonly known as the Whore of Babylon:

"a woman sitting on a scarlet beast which was full of blasphemous names, and it had seven heads and ten horns. The woman was arrayed in purple and scarlet, and bedecked with gold and jewels and pearls, holding in her hand a golden cup full of abominations and the impurities of her fornication; and on her forehead was written a name of mystery: 'Babylon the great, mother of harlots and of earth's abomination.' And I saw the woman, drunk with the blood of the saints and the blood of the martyrs of Jesus."[14]

What has happened in the course of the biblical dream is that a tension within the anima, first revealed in Eve, becomes a cleavage represented by two types of women: the dutiful daughter and mother type and the loose and wild woman seductress type. The one pulls toward Yahweh and the spiritual, the other away from Yahweh and toward the sensual and earthy. It is another version of the obedience/disobedience conflict. This cleavage in the anima becomes intensified into a drastic split, represented by the Virgin Mary and the Whore of Babylon. Mary represents the extreme of the spiritual anima supporting radical idealism, while the Whore of Babylon represents the most extreme opposition possible to the spiritual ideal – debauched sensuality allied with evil. The historical consequences of this extreme tension in the anima have been with us in Western European culture now for nearly two thousand years. On the one hand, we have a highly spiritual culture with refined ideals and political and social movements to support them, monasticism, a

---

[14] Revelation 17:3-6.

celibate clergy, a strong cultural emphasis on caring for the weak and poor, artistic standards of great refinement, etc.; on the other, we have an equivalent extreme of pollution on all levels of society and culture, the political evils of dictatorship and mass psychopathy, the brutality of rampant capitalism, child pornography, etc. There has been an eternal and unremitting battle between these two extremes in the anima, the former identified with God and the good, and the latter with evil. We still await a resolution of this stressful inner division.

LECTURE SIX
Animus Images

When we speak of anima images as we did in the previous lecture, whether in the Bible or elsewhere such as in dreams, in myth, in fairy tales, or in projection, we are generally speaking about the psychology of men; that is, the masculine side of the human species. To speak of the animus and of animus figures shifts our focus of attention to the psychology of women. The animus is the corresponding inner structure in women — the aspect of a woman's personality that interfaces between ego-consciousness and the unconscious. The animus compensates and compliments the persona of women. Since women are typically constellated in their personality development with a persona that has "feminine" features, the animus will have a masculine cast to it and be represented by men in dreams, projection and fantasy. The anima and the animus are the tools, or functions, with which we relate to the unconscious.

In this lecture I will propose that we consider the Bible as the dream of the female element in the psyche of the people who are elaborating and manifesting the Yahweh archetype in history, namely the Chosen People, the Hebrews. In fact, this makes a lot of sense since often in the Bible, Israel is spoken of as the bride of Yahweh. She is dreaming Yahweh. This will be our perspective in this lecture.

Let's see if this approach has something interesting to tell us about the biblical dream.

Jung speaks of the anima and animus as archetypes, that is, as forms of psychic energy arising from the collective unconscious and impacting consciousness and the personal unconscious. If we look at the biblical text as a dream and we see that the primary archetype seeking full expression in ego-consciousness is Yahweh, the Great Father and law-giver and boundary setter, we could well suppose, at least for the sake of argument, that this is an animus dream. As Jung speaks of the animus, it is the image of the father, and it corresponds to the "paternal Logos"[15]; it is made up of philosophical and religious ideas and the attitude resulting from them[16]; it is a psychopomp, a mediator, Logos. "The animus gives to woman's consciousness a capacity for reflection, deliberation, and self-knowledge."[17] When the animus is not very well integrated into ego-consciousness, or when it is repressed or held back and left undeveloped, it comes out in an individual or a collective body typically in stubborn opinions, absolute statements, and poorly thought-out generalizations.

It makes sense to think of the biblical dream as being as much the product of woman's unconscious as man's, and that the image of Yahweh is therefore a conflation of man-dreamed and woman-dreamed elements, the two merging in the course of the tradition and being woven together into a single narrative. For present purposes in this lecture we will consider the biblical dream from the viewpoint of the

---

[15] C.G. Jung, *Aion*, in *CW.* 9ii, par. 29.
[16] Ibid., 33.
[17] Ibid.

female dreamer and look on Yahweh and other male figures in the dream as animus images.

In Yahweh we have the Great Father image, and in such figures as Moses, the various kings, and especially the prophets, we see mediating figures – psychopomps. For purposes of orientation, I have selected five women in the biblical dream to represent the dream ego, that is, the image of the dreaming subject: Eve, Zipporah, Job's wife, Mary, and the pregnant woman of Revelation. This will be the feminine line upon which we will hang our interpretation of animus revelation and evolution in the biblical dream. Each of these figures, in turn, will be seen in a context that includes: 1) the woman subject, 2) her masculine partner or husband, 3) the archetypal animus, and 4) the Chthonic Mother. We will look at five such sets, which stretch from beginning to end of the biblical dream. By considering what happens in these five four-fold structures, we can see what is going on in the feminine psyche of the people as portrayed in the biblical dream.

The first set-up consists of Eve as subject, Adam as her mate, Yahweh as the archetypal animus figure, and the serpent as representative of the Chthonic Mother. In these initial sequences of the biblical dream series, we see that the feminine subject, Eve, is somewhat aware of the presence of Yahweh as an archetypal animus, but not directly related or greatly committed to Him. Her husband, Adam, is closer to Yahweh, while she is still quite attached to the Chthonic Mother. She listens to the serpent, not to Yahweh. So at this stage, while the archetypal animus has made its appearance as a personality of force and power, its impact upon the subject is somewhat weak and limited. On balance, the claims of the Chthonic Mother outweigh the claims of the archetypal Father.

Nevertheless, the Yahweh figure is clearly in charge of the power equation, exacting His consequences in no uncertain terms. His power is not to be denied. In this regard, we would assume that Yahweh compensates for the subject's too close attachment to the Chthonic Mother, forcing Eve to separate from Her. The animus is demanding separation from the Mother archetype, then also insists on submission to the relationship with the husband, Adam, and to the suffering that comes with living in the ego world of time and space and of mortality. The eternal cyclic rhythms of Mother Nature are replaced with a sense of linear time, in which birth and death occurs and tragedy is likely. Attachment to the Mother is weakened and attachment to the Father is strengthened. This creates a dynamic that we call history.

Eve soon gives birth to two sons, Cain and Abel. Among her few words in the text are, "I have gotten a man with the help of the Lord,"[18] spoken upon giving birth to her first child, Cain. Later she will give birth to a third son, Seth, to replace the murdered Abel. As a mother, Eve is mainly the mother of men, again a signal that the dream is emphasizing the influx of animus elements into the subject's consciousness. The Bible, from this point of view, will turn out to be the story of how the feminine subject comes to terms with the archetypal animus as it impinges more and more powerfully upon her consciousness and insists on a place, on integration.

We leap ahead in the dream sequence now to Zipporah. Zipporah is not a well-known figure in the biblical narrative,

---

[18] Genesis 4:1.

but she is important for our purposes because she is the wife of Moses. When Moses flees Egypt, he comes to the land of Midian and ends up marrying Zipporah, the daughter of the priest variously called Reuel or Jethro. Zipporah bears Moses a son named Gershom, playing on the Hebrew *ger*, "sojourner." In this set-up, Zipporah is the central subject, Moses is the husband figure, Yahweh is the archetypal animus who is also honored and supported by her father Jethro, and the Chthonic Mother is indicated by the mysterious figure, an "angel" or demon, who attacks Moses and nearly kills him on the way home from his vision on Mt. Sinai.

The central figure in this drama, Zipporah, is a father's daughter, and her mother is not mentioned. Her father, a priest of Midian, is considered to be a priest in an early Yahwistic cult. The origin of Yahwistic religion is generally placed in the area of Midian, where Mt. Horeb is located. This is Yahweh's mountain and is where He met Moses in the burning bush and later gave him the Ten Commandments. Mt. Horeb, or Mt. Sinai, is the mountain of revelation, the place where the archetypal animus reveals his identity: "I AM WHO I AM."[19] This name indicates the Lord's freedom and autonomy, as well as His power. He is sovereign and does not need to answer to anyone. He is the Absolute. His appearance as a fire is also noteworthy as an animus image. The animus, defined by Jung as spirit, is portrayed by flames that leap upward. From time immemorial, the leaping flame has symbolized the spirit, and it will do so again in the New Testament on the day of Pentecost when tongues of fire dance over the heads of the apostles gathered for prayer in the upper room. Moses, Zipporah's husband, receives his

---

[19] Exodus 3:14.

97

vocation from the animus, her father's archetypal source of majesty and power. It is the case that the father of a woman receives his power in her life by virtue of an animus projection, as does her husband. She will submit to them freely and lovingly if they behave according to the archetypal prescriptions because they radiate the divine energy of the archetypal animus.

Zipporah is with Moses at Mt. Horeb when he experiences his encounter with "I AM." The critical importance of her presence is not evident, however, until they set out to return home. On the journey, "at a lodging place," the text says, "the Lord met him [i.e., Moses] and sought to kill him. Then Zipporah took a flint and cut off her son's foreskin, and touched Moses' feet with it, and said, 'Surely you are a bridegroom of blood to me!' So he let him alone."[20] This passage has puzzled scholars. Who is the "Lord"? If it is Yahweh, why would he be trying to kill Moses whom he has just commissioned to go to Egypt and free the Hebrews? If not Yahweh, then who? And what does the expression, "Surely you are a bridegroom of blood to me!" have to do with anything? Why does this and the act of presenting her son's circumcised foreskin have the power to ward off the demonic killer? My speculation, based on our psychological inter-pretation, is that the killer demon is a derivative of the Chthonic Mother, earlier represented in the Garden of Eden as a serpent. This demon is hostile to Yahweh and to Yahweh's recently anointed servant, Moses, and Zipporah is able to protect Moses because of a secret connection that she enjoys to the Chthonic Mother: by claiming Moses as her bride-groom of blood, she exorcises the demon. In this gesture,

---

[20] Exodus 4:24-26.

Zipporah has cast her lot with the archetypal animus against the Chthonic Mother and has separated herself from Her decisively.

In Zipporah, we see a much more animus-inclined ego-consciousness of woman than in Eve. She is able to act for her husband, and she takes an active interventionist stance against the force that would destroy Moses and undermine the influence of Yahweh in the course of history. Because of Zipporah, we have the Judeo-Christian tradition, which is critically mediated by her husband Moses. Her husband becomes the psychopomp for a whole people, mediating to them the will of Yahweh in the form of the Ten Commandments and leading them out of Egypt (the Great Mother) to the promised land. It would not be too much to say, from the viewpoint of the perspective we are taking regarding the animus, that Moses' prophetic role and identity are created by Zipporah's archetypal animus, which is allied with her father complex.

Moses, Zipporah's husband, receives his divine vocation and his direction from the God whom he discovered in the land of his father-in-law, Jethro, the priest of Midian. Through the influence of Zipporah, he is led into the proximity of the archetypal animus force in the background of this culture and initiated into its priesthood on Mount Horeb. Zipporah then protects him from attack on the road home after this initiatory experience.

The influence of a woman over her husband often does, in fact, effect something like this. Through a process that is quite unconscious and referred to technically by Jung as "induction" or "influence" and by object relations theorists as projective identification, the husband's new identity as a man is strongly affected by the woman's archetypal animus, usually as mediated by her father complex. Husbands know that they are in competition with the wife's father – than whom no man is greater! – but it is not her actual father that is the giant of masculine prowess looming over him through her unconscious projections and expectations, but her father as invested with the archetypal force and magnitude of the animus. This constellates in a man a new level of manhood. In the case of Moses, it made him a prophet of Yahweh and vastly increased his stature. And for the wife, Zipporah, she now has a husband who more closely resembles her father and behind him the archetypal animus, Yahweh.

Zipporah's commitment to the animus is stronger than Eve's. In the case of Eve, the feminine subject is still seriously open to temptation from the Chthonic Mother, the serpent, the world of the Great Goddess. Zipporah is not. By the time we reach the exodus in our biblical dream, the feminine subject has shifted allegiance fully to the archetypal animus. This is subtly reflected also in the actions of Moses' mother, his sister Miriam, and Pharaoh's daughter, all of whom conspire to advance the cause of the spiritual animus, Yahweh, over the claims of the Mother-bound, polytheistic Egyptians. Moses the law-giver is saved, constellated, and supported by irrationally committed women, and this tradition has continued throughout the history of Judeo-Christian history in the common knowledge that this seemingly rather anti-feminine, patriarchal religion has been carried and passed on through the generations by its women and mothers.

If given to a paranoid cast of mind, one could suspect that the entire history of this tradition is an unconscious conspiracy on the part of women to make men conform to their animus constellations and expectations. Certainly values like monogamy, strong emotional bondedness between fathers and children, sensitivity to widows and orphans – all values that in other religions, like the Greek for instance, would be associated with Goddesses and their cults rather than with Gods and theirs – have been centrally woven into this tradition and enunciated as the values of Yahweh through his male prophets and spokesmen from Moses to Jesus and Paul. But this commitment on the part of the feminine subject to the animus has also caused a problem for her. This is the occlusion of her relation to the Chthonic Mother archetype, which stands prior to and behind the animus archetype. To "get out of the mother," the feminine subject had to commit herself firmly to the animus, to Yahweh over the serpent and Egypt, but this in turn has tended to embed the feminine subject in the animus to the point of nearly losing contact with the feminine archetype of the self. By committing so strongly to the archetypal animus and investing the husband with its authority and energy ("numinosity" – Moses' face shines when he descends from Mt. Sinai after talking with Yahweh there), it turns out that the husband's position becomes more and more dominant. He gets all the credit. And while she may benefit from it, she also suffers from it. One can read the story of Job as an attempt to redress the balance somewhat by putting the husband in his place.

Following Jung, we can read the Book of Job as the midpoint in the long dream that is the Bible. We might also consider it as a dream from midlife, when the ego position and persona have been consolidated and the life cycle takes a turn toward greater acceptance of psychic elements that have been neglected and left out. The kingdom has been established. Job and his wife have worked hard, produced seven sons and three daughters, and now they can watch them grow and prosper as they themselves have done. The Lord is in his heaven, and all is right with the world. Only there is trouble brewing in heaven. Satan tempts God to test his servant Job, and God succumbs, allowing Satan to rain down on his head disaster upon disaster until all is destroyed and he sits broken among the ashes and scrapes his loathsome sores with a potsherd. "Then his wife said to him, 'Do you still hold fast your integrity? Curse God, and die.'"[21] This is Job's wife's only appearance in the book. She is not even named. And yet the calamity that befell Job must have equally touched her, perhaps even more than it did him. She is anonymous and practically silent. Her despair is uttered in those simple words: "Curse God, and die."

Let's consider this as her dream. The set-up here is Job's wife as feminine subject, Job as her husband, Yahweh as the archetypal animus, and Satan represented as the serpent, the Chthonic Mother. In the world of consciousness, things are at first peaceful and settled. But in the depths of the unconscious there is a conflict. Yahweh seems to be in charge, as He should be, having previously consolidated His power, first with His appearance in Genesis, then through His revelation of the law to Moses, and later in His leadership of the Hebrews through the wilderness and into the promised land where the kingdom was conquered, a political system established, and a temple built. Throughout, the feminine subject has become largely cooperative: supplying sons, saving the lives of heroes, even herself taking up the heroic sword occasionally as in the case of Deborah and Jael. She has been committed to this development. Mostly. But what

---

[21] Job 2:9.

about the left-out Chthonic Mother? By the time we get to the story of Job, the Chthonic Mother/serpent has taken on the appearance of a servant of Yahweh's, a mere messenger going up and down the earth and spying for Him, and the feminine subject has become anonymous and without a name. Yahweh's goal has been achieved and complacency sets in. Job thought that he would die in his comfortable bed surrounded by his children and grandchildren, "my glory fresh with me, and my bow ever new in my hand,"[22] as he says the time for midlife crisis has arrived.

Jung calls Satan "God's doubting thought,"[23] but perhaps we can think of Satan as the restless, unsatisfied, and by now pretty resentful and envy-filled eye of the Chthonic Mother.

When God gives Satan permission to destroy Job's possessions and to kill his children, he draws a line, "...upon himself do not put forth your hand,"[24] without mention of Job's wife. Yet she is not touched physically. In sparing her, Satan shows some connection to her since he does this out of his own will rather than at God's beheast. The main task is to test Job, the husband. Job's wife despairs under the onslaught and bitterly advises her husband to give up his trustful and confident attitude toward this so-called spiritual father of theirs. But this her husband will not do, and from his bold resistance to her advice springs the ensuing story and its ultimate resolution. It is the story of his transformation and of the beginning of God's as well.

When Jung published his major work on the Bible, *Answer to Job*, he was roundly criticized from all quarters.

[22] Job 29:20.
[23] C.G. Jung, *Answer to Job*, in *CW* 11, par. 579.
[24] Job 1:12.

103

His argument was that Job was justified in taking the position he did: Job was righteous and God was in the wrong, morally, for playing around with a human life in this way. Yahweh is shown to be the one in need of further moral development. Basically, Jung says that Yahweh is confronting a superior, more conscious figure in Job and loses the moral contest, although He certainly has the capacity to overwhelm a mere man with his power and authority. In His heart of hearts, when He consults His wisdom (Sophia), Yahweh knows that he must change and become more conscious, more sensitive, and more loving, and so His confrontation with Job actually sets in motion the story that culminates in the incarnation of Himself in His Son, in the birth, life and death of Jesus.

Fr. Victor White attacked Jung for siding with Job. White takes the more traditional position that the story is about the undue self-righteousness and pride of a man coming up against the superior force of life and of God. Job discovers his humility and bows before the superior authority of God. This is a story, White argues using Jungian psychology, of the ego's relativization. He criticizes Jung for inflating the ego by supporting Job, instead of recognizing the ego's defeat at the hands of the self.

If we consider this as an animus story, however, we can have it both ways. It is true that the husband, who represents an approximation of the incarnation of the animus, is humbled and relativized by this confrontation with the archetypal animus. The animus is greater and stronger and more original than the husband, who is a mere approximation and a Johnny-come-lately (as most wives can readily attest about their husbands). But it is also true that the animus, Yahweh, has been tricked by Satan into a confrontation that leaves him unsatisfied and morally defeated. Yahweh had not asked for this kind of a serious personal confrontation with the husband, Job. He was only experimenting. But now He is held accountable. He has shown His face directly. He has become more conscious through this confrontation with the husband, and in this revelation the animus has been brought down a peg, has been relativized. He may lay down the law and set up standards of moral perfection for others to follow, but He doesn't actually live up to them himself. This is humiliating. So in this confrontation between the husband and the archetypal animus, instigated by the spirit of malevolence from the repressed and denied Chthonic Mother, we see that consciousness is produced and the animus does come closer to the human – closer to integration into ego-consciousness. During temper tantrums and outbursts, the unconscious, or repressed and withheld attitudes that lie behind the neat and well-adjusted persona, come out into the open and can then be examined. This is the condition for transformation. The material has to come out.

If we can see the first appearance of the archetypal animus in the story of Eve, his further revelation and consolidation in the story of Zipporah, and his relativization through consciousness in the story of Job's wife, then we see his transformation in the story of Mary. We also see in her quite a significant change in the feminine subject as well as in the husband figure. In this story, we find the centrality of the feminine subject in a way that has not been characteristic of the other figures discussed so far. After the anonymity of Job's wife, Mary looks like a celebrity, a star. Her name is prominent, lit up. The quaternity in this part of the Biblical dream is Mary as feminine subject, Joseph as the husband figure, God as archetypal animus, and Satan in the role of the Chthonic Mother. Satan is placed in this role because of the earlier dream material, ultimately from the initial dream in Genesis, where the Chthonic Mother is more directly represented by the serpent. But we must be consistent in tracing the line of the Chthonic Mother and her influence through the text: she is the left-out, fourth element and appears in the text either as the seductive sexual woman (Delilah, Bathsheba), as goddess-worshipping religions and their sacred figures (Egypt, Baal, the pig), or disguised (the serpent, the demon, Satan, the dragon, Antichrist). There are other positive women figures in the biblical dream, of course, and in this portion of it, the Gospels, there are a number of important ones: Elizabeth, Mary's cousin; Mary and Martha, the sisters of Lazarus; and Mary Magdalene who gives up her sinful ways and comes over to the Lord. These, however, we must, for purposes of this interpretation, consider to be persona figures, i.e., ideals for the feminine subject or supportive of her conscious position visa-vis the conscious world. Were the Chthonic Mother to appear, we would expect an Oriental Goddess like Ishtar or Isis or the maternal Artemis of Ephesus. We do not get such positive images of the Chthonic Mother because she is being rather heavily repressed in favor of the archetypal animus, Yahweh, and so she appears in disguise and mostly in negative form.

The most prominent figures in the Mary quaternity are in somewhat striking contrast to the quaternity consisting of Job's wife, her husband, Yahweh, and Satan. Here, the feminine subject is the star (Mary) and the husband figure has become almost as anonymous as the feminine subject in the Job's wife configuration. The Chthonic Mother element, Satan, flits about here and there and is certainly extremely powerful in its effects, but works mostly by an invisible hand as he/she generates resistances and murderous effects by infiltrating the population. It is by comparing the feminine subject figures and the husband figures that we can see most clearly the development from the point in the dream where we met Job's wife to this point of Mary's appearance and her mysterious *coniunctio* with the archetypal animus, the Holy Spirit. Mary is the only feminine subject figure in the entire biblical dream that has a direct contact like this with the archetypal animus. In all other cases, this has been mediated through the husband figure, who takes on the coloration and magnitude and some of the numinosum of the animus but is not the animus fully. In Mary's case, however, the husband is diminutive, reduced in size to the role of a servant. Her primary *coniunctio* is with the archetypal animus, and the child she bears is a product of that union.

Her son, Jesus, being a child of the union with the animus, is of a highly spiritual nature, the animus being pure spirit. He stands in for the animus in this quaternity, since he is, after all, the Son of God. It is precisely this *coniunctio* directly with the archetypal animus that gives this feminine subject her immense value. Mary is a humble woman who by virtue of her animus connection is elevated from the status of humble servant girl to *theotokos*, God-bearer. And in her famous song, the Magnificat, she indicates her consciousness of this elevation: "My soul magnifies the Lord, and my spirit rejoices in God my Savior, for he has regarded the low estate of his handmaiden. For behold, henceforth all generations will call me blessed; for he who is might has done great things for me, and holy is his name."[25] The feminine subject

---

[25] Luke 1:46-49.

has been redeemed from obscurity and anonymity and is now elevated in her own self-value above the husband figure. This is evident compensation from the unconscious and could threaten an inflation, which may be the reason that Jesus puts her down so much. The quaternity that results from Mary's *coniunctio* with the archetypal animus does not actually remove the husband figure, but it does remove animus projections from him. He is thoroughly human and stands in relation to the feminine subject as a dutiful, perhaps too dutiful, husband. Jesus stands in for the archetypal animus, to be sure, a more human version, but still highly numinous and certainly for her, a *fascinosum*. She asks him to turn water into wine at the marriage in Cana, and he does so, but not before making a caustic remark: "O woman, what have you to do with me."[26] (John 2:4). With a son like this, even though he is magical, she is unlikely to get too inflated! He may be a closer and more human animus figure than God the Father, but he is still autonomous.

The danger of inflation is that the ego identifies with an archetype and loses its own specific identity. The archetype becomes incarnated badly in this way and loses its usefulness and its positive compensatory effect in the conscious world. So, these texts that look so harsh and down-putting are actually guardians of the process and its deeper intentions. Were Mary to become inflated with her position – the wife of God, the mother of God – she would go insane, become psychotic, and the role of Jesus in history would be swallowed up in madness. The dream text, therefore, carefully preserves a high enough value for the feminine subject, exalts her position certainly from where it was in earlier

---

[26] John 2:4.

portions of the biblical dream, shows her to be a highly spiritual person with a clear and unambiguous commitment to the archetypal animus, but still preserves her from becoming inflated through identifying too closely with her Messianic offspring.

When a woman achieves this position in real life, she values herself (her ego) highly enough but she does not take credit for all of her wisdom, inspiration, and spiritual insight. She can speak with the tongues of men and angels but still stay human; she can be wise but still love; she can know the stars and the most lofty ideals and still remain empathic with a broken and imperfect world. Most of what her animus has to offer will be despised and rejected. Her prophetic pronouncements will set teeth on edge causing consternation and opposition. She will run into the resistance of a collective that in no way sees it her way. And this spiritual attitude will be crushed by the weight of history. For all of her wisdom, her rhetoric, her sacrificial acts in the name of love and charity, her spiritual brilliance, tragedy will occur and she will see her dreams crucified.

Next to the image of Mary giving birth in Bethlehem, it is the picture of her at the foot of the cross and holding her broken, charismatic son in her lap that has gripped the Western imagination. In this part of the narrative, the feminine subject experiences the loss of her dream. Eve saw one son kill another, Job's wife knew the grief of losing all ten of her children, and Mary is forced to look upon the cruel crucifixion of her godlike son at the instigation of a vicious, ignorant, angry mob. Surely this experience of lost children over the centuries must have produced a saltiness of wisdom about life in this feminine subject. If individuation leads to wisdom through the conflict of the opposites, as Jung said,[27] then this feminine subject, Mary, standing at the foot of the cross upon which her son was crucified, must represent an opportunity for the profoundest wisdom. The opposites that came together and produced this collision on Golgotha were the archetypal animus Yahweh and His son Jesus on one side and the Chthonic Mother and her minion Satan on the other. This is the story in the background, which is most starkly portrayed in the gospel of John and in the Book of Revelation. Mary at the foot of the cross portrays a culmination of the conflict between the forces that are first represented in the Garden of Eden and that thread their way through the entire dream text. Here we see the feminine subject, Mary, standing in the midst of the conflict, at the point of greatest tension, and then bearing Jesus in another sense as she holds him in the position of the famous Pieta. At this point of tension, a new religion is born, and the cross is its symbol. Mary standing at the foot of the cross is the mother of this religion, and for this reason she has held such an important place in its iconography and imagery, if not always in its theology. Mary is the first Christian.

In the Book of Revelation, there is another quaternity with a feminine subject. This figure is referred to as "the woman with child,"[28] and the description of her is exalted and archetypal. She may be the closest image there is in the Bible to a goddess figure: she is "a woman clothed with the sun, with the moon under her feet, and on her head a crown of twelve stars."[29] In iconography Mary is sometimes

---

[27] C.G. Jung, *Mysterium Coniunctionis*, *CW* 14, paras. 330-36.
[28] Revelation 12:1.
[29] Ibid.

portrayed as this woman. She is pregnant and gives birth to a male child "who is to rule all the nations with a rod of iron." Both this woman and her child are threatened by "a great red dragon, with seven heads and seven horns, and seven diadems upon his heads."[30] The woman, after giving birth to the son, flees into the wilderness where she has a place prepared by God, and the child "is caught up to God and to his throne."[31] In a mere six verses this account is presented as "a great portent," auguring the future.

Jung, in *Answer to Job*, looks upon this figure and her son as preparatory to the next stage in the evolution of this religious tradition. For our purposes here, we can see that it presents a quaternity that is somewhat continuous with the others we have looked at, and is also, in some ways, radically different. In this quaternity, the feminine subject is exalted indeed, to the position of a cosmic figure, a sort of sky goddess with the sun as her raiment, the moon as her standpoint, and stars in her hair. Yet she certainly is not omnipotent; she remains vulnerable to the red dragon, a further representation of the Chthonic Mother from the serpent in the garden of Eden. The dragon and the whore of Babylon are more or less synonymous figures. The son is, of course, a new version of Jesus, a recapitulation on the heavenly plane, as it were. The husband is not evident in this quaternio, and one assumes that God is the father, as in the earlier version of Mary and her pregnancy. The disappearance of the husband and of the human element tells us that this is a dream whose time has not yet come. It is, as the text says, a prefiguration of a future development, and in that

---

[30] Revelation 12:3.
[31] Revelation 12:5.

development the son will rule with a rod of iron.[32] This would seem to indicate a future development in the feminine subject of a masterful heroic animus, but at a more this-worldly, historical, and political level. The rod will be of iron and meant to rule. While the tone of this passage may be punitive and harsh, there is also the premonition of a more worldly, less spiritual incarnation.

In the meantime, the feminine subject is protected in a place prepared for her by God. Her features and the presence of sun, moon, and stars would seem to auger wholeness and integration on her part. I believe she is a prefiguration of a possibility for feminine wholeness, in which the strong antagonisms between Chthonic Mother and spiritual father, body and spirit (animus), will have settled into a more harmonious relation. It is an image of promise during a time that is heavily conflicted and unpropitious otherwise. Perhaps she has waited for our time to become manifest.

---

[32] Ibid.

Election and Adoption – Envy and the Self

From the accumulated experience in working with dreams and long dream series, Jungian analysts know that repeated themes and motifs are especially significant. When a figure appears over and over again, or a particular line of action, or a scene, it is a signal that some content or dynamic is trying to break through into consciousness. The repetitious theme is a call for attention.

In the biblical dream, which is a long series of woven together dream episodes, one theme that recurs in many variations is Yahweh's act of choosing. When Jung compared Yahweh to the Greek gods, he made the point that the crucial difference between them is that Yahweh is personally involved in His creation; it matters to Him how people behave, what they do and how they think. Moreover: "In view of this intense personal relatedness to His chosen people, it was only to be expected that a regular covenant would develop which also extended to certain individuals."[33] Yahweh consequently comes across as a strongly judging and discriminating personality, often emotional and irritable and certainly showing strong preferences. This is an archetype that has something very specific in mind. It is distinctive.

---

[33] C.G. Jung, *Answer to Job*, in *CW* 11, par. 569.

This tendency becomes evident early on in the case of Adam's and Eve's first children, Cain and Abel. Cain, the first-born, is a tiller of the ground, a farmer; his younger brother, Abel, is a shepherd. Both bring offerings to the Lord, the one bringing the first fruits of the earth, the other the firstlings of his flock. "And the Lord had regard for Abel and his offering, but for Cain and his offering he had no regard."[34] The Lord chooses his preferred meal, lamb, at the sacrificial dinner, and like an insensitive father He shows His strong preference for the favored gift over the other offer. Understandably, "Cain was very angry, and his countenance fell." He's the slighted elder son. Wouldn't you suppose a father would prefer his elder child? Instead he prefers the gift of the younger one. This will be typical throughout the narrative: Yahweh will choose in His own fashion and sometimes quite arbitrarily and irrationally so. He knows what He likes and makes His decisions accordingly.

Of course, we must keep in mind that the Lord is not directly the father; that role is occupied by Adam, who does not play a part in this story. Adam is strangely an absent father. The two sons are left exposed directly to the Almighty without parental mediation or protection. There is an absence of defense against the onslaught of the archetype at this early stage in the story. The Lord confronts Cain: "Why are you angry, and why has your countenance fallen? If you do well, will you not be accepted? And if you do not do well, sin is crouching at the door; its desire is for you, but you must master it."[35] These are words that could be taken as an attempt to teach and instruct, even if they suggest a rather

---

[34] Genesis 4:4.
[35] Genesis 4:6.

gruff manner. Cain is chided for feeling angry about the slight from the Lord who ignores his offering, but he is given a chance to recover and is encouraged to resist his anger at his brother. This he cannot do. It festers in him, and the evil that is crouching at the door finds an easy entrance into his heart: "Cain said to Abel his brother, 'Let us go out to the field.' And when they were in the field, Cain rose up against his brother Abel, and killed him."[36] This murder was constellated by the Lord's clear preference for Abel's offering over Cain's. It is an attack inspired by envy. Envy is the inevitable by-product of Yahweh's act of choosing his brother over him.

After the murder, the Lord comes to Cain and asks: "Where is your brother?" And Cain makes the famous reply: "I do not know; am I my brother's keeper?"[37] For his act of murderous rage brought on by envy, Cain is punished: he is made into a wanderer and a fugitive on the earth; the ground will no longer yield to him and no longer produce harvests. He receives the mark of Cain on his forehead. He is a farmer deprived of his land and his living, and he becomes an unhappy, dissatisfied wanderer. As punishment he is deprived even of what was not acceptable in the eyes of the Lord. From now on he will have to envy both the successful farmers and the shepherds. He will have nothing of his own, and he will be shunned by society. What does this kind of splitting mean psychologically, coming so early in our biblical dream narrative?

We know from experience that the initial dreams of a dream series present problems that will recur throughout the series and will require much working through in order

---

[36] Genesis 4:8.
[37] Genesis 4:9.

to resolve. In this story of Cain and Abel, we are presented with a central dynamic in the dreamer's personality that causes trauma, splitting and repression. It results in what we might call a "specialness complex" in the chosen one, which creates the shadow of envy in others. Envy is the evil crouching at the door, and it is murderous.

At one level of reading, the Bible is a family saga (like *Buddenbrooks* by Thomas Mann) extending over generations. At the heart of this family story is the image of a Father who sired many children and then selected His favorites. The sense of this invisible, omnipotent, creative, choosing Father haunts the entire family chronicle. The theme of chosenness is the Bible's most crucial theme. Everything else hinges on the Father's choosing. Out of the dynamic created by this proclivity on the invisible Father's part arises jealousy, sibling rivalry, and ultimately, envy and murderous attacks on the chosen ones. "The chosen" is the one who has a privileged position in relation to the source of creation and sustenance. Ultimately, the chosen one becomes so closely and intimately identified with the source of life and goodness that he becomes one with Him, as we see in the story of Jesus. And this leaves the other siblings "out," with no alternative but to envy. Since envy is going to play such an important part in the biblical dream series, we need to pause for a moment and consider its psychology.

In a searching and vividly written book entitled *Mal Occhio*, Lawrence DiStasi recalls the tactics used by his Italian grandparents to guard against the malevolent impact of the "evil eye." Most typical was for parents to avoid boasting to strangers about their children. The fear of stimulating envy among others guided their caution. Because healthy, beautiful children were so highly prized, they became the chief targets of envy attacks. Should a child become suddenly and unaccountably ill, the working of an evil eye was instantly suspected, and a counter-sorcerer would be enlisted to speak some healing incantations and to counteract the sickening effects of the envy attack. In thinking about the psychology of envy, it is important to note that in DiStasi's account children were the most frequent targets. A child would draw the attention of an evil eye not so much because of economic or genealogical advantages but because the child symbolizes the self, the highest value, the "treasure hard to attain." In this we see the picture of the ego's envy of the self.

It may seem paradoxical to speak of the ego's envy of the self, since both would seem to belong to oneself, yet this does seem to be the case of what envy essentially is. "Envy," from the Latin *invidere*, means "to look into" with hostile intensity. The envious eye is attracted by objects that capture a projection of great worth, of the highest value. In envy, what is perceived in the other is some important aspect of the self, one that it does not possess internally. What the envious eye sees is a supremely valuable aspect of the self. One that, by its location in someone else, deprives the subject of direct access to it. The inner void that is produced by this projection generates hatred and destructiveness, emotions that are central to envy's destructive energy. It is the ego's envy of the self, from which it has been alienated and is perceived externally in projected form, that creates such profound despair and deadly malevolence. Envy is an alarming signal of rupture in the ego-self relation. This is what we see in Cain.

The stimulation of envy is a signal of an important need that is rooted in a legitimate hunger for full selfhood. Envy should not be seen fundamentally as an expression of a dark, destructive side of the self, the archetypal shadow, or blank evil. Once constellated, however, envy can become chronic and come into alliance with the dark side of the self. Then, instead of aiming at wholeness, it converts individuation energy into destructiveness for its own sake, without balance from the self's constructive, creative energies. This is the tragedy of envy. It is perfectly personified by Iago who brings about the destruction of Othello out of envy.

From the beginning of the biblical dream onward, Yahweh is shown as preferring and choosing His favorites, and as things develop, this results in explicit promises and a contractual arrangement called the covenant. The covenant is made up of all of Yahweh's promises to what turns out to be His chosen people, as well as their commitment to honor Him as their sole God. Both sides have chosen to be exclusive in their love and commitment. It is a kind of marriage contract. But even before it comes to that point, Yahweh makes choices that shape the narrative's history and direction. He protects Noah, and after the flood He promises not to destroy the earth again. He singles Abraham and his wife Sarah out from the peoples of earth at that time, and He calls Abraham forth to "the land that I will show you." To Abraham, he makes many promises: riches, a multitude of children, success in every way. And in the sequence of dreams that make up the story of Abraham, we observe Yahweh keeping His word and gradually, often against great odds (like Sarah's advanced age and lack of children!), these promises come to fulfillment.

In the course of this story about the first really great father of the people of Israel, we see Yahweh making some hard decisions as He separates the genetic line of Abraham out from the rest and sets it on its way into history. One of

these is the decision to abandon Ishmael and his mother
Hagar. Here again, Yahweh's decisiveness in creating precisely
the line He wants results in rejection and the creation of an
outcast. Ishmael is, by tradition, the father of the Arab
peoples with whom the children of Abraham continue to
struggle in a seemingly endless deadlock of envy and mutual
suspicion. But the covenant does not include any children
other than those of Sarah. It is Sarah's wish that Hagar and
her son, Ishmael, be driven out of the camp, "for the son of
this slave woman shall not be heir with my son Isaac."
Abraham is upset and does not want to comply, "But God
said to Abraham, 'Be not displeased because of the lad and
because of your slave woman; whatever Sarah says to you,
do as she tells you, for through Isaac shall your descendants
be named. And I will make a nation of the son of the slave
woman also, because he is your offspring.'"[38] Yahweh tries
to let Abraham off the hook of having to choose between his
two sons by telling him that everything will be alright with
the cast off one, but clearly this child of the servant – again,
the older son – is going to come in second best. Isaac, the
son of Sarah, has the inside track.

The role of the mother in selecting the favorite is
noteworthy. Yahweh tells Abraham to do as Sarah tells him.
The mother will play a crucial role again in the case of Jacob
and Esau, where the younger son, Jacob, is preferred by his
mother, Rebekah, to his elder brother. The two brothers are
twins, and while Rebekah is pregnant she "went to inquire
of the Lord. And the Lord said to her, 'two nations are in
your womb, and two peoples, born of you, shall be divided;
the one shall be stronger than the other, the elder shall serve

[38] Genesis 21:12.

the younger.'"[39] Esau is born ahead of Jacob and so by right should have been the heir of his father's property. But Rebekah, remembering the words of the Lord and presumably also following her own irrational preference in the matter as well, sees to it that the prophecy is fulfilled: she disguises Jacob as the elder brother, who is an accomplished hunter, and takes him in to the blind and dying father, Isaac, for the final blessing. Isaac innocently falls into the trap: "See, the smell of my son is as the smell of a field which the Lord has blessed! May God give you of the dew of heaven, and of the fatness of the earth, and plenty of grain and wine. Let peoples serve you, and nations bow down to you. Be lord over your brothers, and may your mother's sons bow down to you. Cursed be everyone who curses you, and blessed be everyone who blesses you!"[40] Unwittingly, Isaac thus carries out the secret will of Yahweh, which is to run the line of inheritance through Jacob. Another disgruntled brother is created – Esau. Esau goes off and marries into Ishmael's tribe, thus creating an alliance against the Lord's chosen, Jacob.

In the marvelous stories of Joseph, the theme of the special son is again a central feature. Joseph, the youngest son of Jacob (by now called Israel), is set against his brothers through his father's special favoritism. In this respect, Jacob is modeled on Yahweh. Israel gives him a coat of many colors: "when his brothers saw that their father loved him more than all his brothers, they hated him, and could not speak peaceably to him."[41] Again, murderous envy is stirred up in

---

[39] Genesis 25:22-23.
[40] Genesis 27:27-29.
[41] Genesis 37:4.

the hearts of the rejected brothers, and the evil that crouches at the door springs onto center stage as they dispose of the golden child by selling him into slavery. As things turn out, of course, Joseph not only prospers in Egypt, but turns out to be the savior of his family. Elevated to the role of prince in Egypt, he insures the survival of the genetic line in a time of drought and famine. In the irrational preference of father Israel for Joseph, we see an imitation of Yahweh's irrational preference for certain individuals over others.

The covenant that ultimately binds the tribes of Israel (descendant of the twelve sons of Jacob) into a single unit is forged between Yahweh and this people through the mediation of Moses, Israel's greatest prophet and spiritual father. The classic text of the covenant is found in Deuteronomy, chapters 27- 33. Here, Moses and the elders of Israel call the people together and explain the contract: the Israelites are to obey the law as it has been given by Yahweh through Moses, and in exchange for this obedience, "the Lord your God will set you high above all the nations of the earth."[42] This extraordinary promise is spelled out in detail: increase in cattle and flocks, plenty of grain for bread, defeat of enemies, and general prosperity and many children.

"The Lord will establish you as a people holy to Himself, as He has sworn to you, if you keep the commandments of the Lord your God, and walk in his ways. And all the peoples of the earth shall see that you are called by the name of the Lord; and they shall be afraid of you... The Lord will open to you his good treasury the heavens, to give the rain of your land in its season and to bless all the work of your hands; and you shall lend to many nations, but you shall not

---

[42] Deuteronomy 28:1.

borrow. And the Lord will make you the head, and not the tail; and you shall tend upward only, and not downward, if you obey the commandments of the Lord your God, which I command you this day, being careful to do them, and if you do not turn aside from any of the words which I command you this day, to the right hand or to the left, to go after other gods to serve them."[43]

These promises are followed by a series of ferocious threats of punishment for disobedience. The punishments described are as grim as the blessings are pleasing: "the foreigner who comes from a far land, would say, when they see the afflictions of that land and the sicknesses with which the Lord has made it sick – the whole land brimstone and salt, and a burnt-out waste, unsown, and growing nothing, where no grass can sprout…"[44]

Yahweh also promises King David to uphold his side of the covenant. In the poetic words of the psalmist, Yahweh reiterates his faithfulness to his chosen:

> "He shall cry to me, 'Thou art my Father,
>   my God, and the Rock of my salvation.'
> And I will make him the first-born,
>   the highest of the kings of the earth.
> My steadfast love I will keep for him forever,
>   and my covenant will stand firm for him.
> I will establish his line forever,
>   and his throne as the days of the heavens."[45]

---

[43] Deuteronomy 28:9-14.
[44] Deuteronomy 29:22-23.
[45] Psalms 89:27-29.

It is on the ground of Yahweh's urging, choosing, promising, threatening, and cajoling that the chosen people idea is forged and maintained throughout the biblical dream. Yahweh is clearly the director of this family drama, the dreaming self that is guiding the process.

This notion of specialness and chosenness carries over powerfully into the New Testament and is reiterated many times in the narratives of the Gospels and by Paul. Out of this affirmation, a serious problem develops as Jesus replaces David as the chosen one. Baptized by John in the Jordan, "he came up out of the water, [and] immediately saw the heavens opened and the Spirit descending upon him like a dove; and a voice came from heaven, 'Thou are my beloved Son; with thee I am well pleased.'"[46] Yahweh is choosing another pathway for His revelation and incarnation in history. Now Jesus is the favored son. Obviously something has happened to Yahweh. He is signaling a new direction.

As Jesus emerges on the scene and makes his claims, he calls down upon himself the wrath of the displaced elder brothers. Jesus is standing in the position of the chosen, just like Abel, Isaac, Joseph, David. The established leaders of Israel in the Sanhedrin are placed into the role of Cain, Ishmael, and Joseph's disgruntled elder brothers who seethe with envy. The force motivating the priests and Pharisees to stir up the mob against Jesus is envy: the specialness of the people and their privileged position in history by virtue of the covenant is being directly challenged by an upstart young brother figure, and if they lost their position, their most central and deeply felt connection to the self would go along with it.

---

[46] Mark 1:10-11.

As New Testament thought evolves, the notion develops of adoption into the new community through baptism. With the figure of Jesus Christ (spiritual Messiah), the biblical dream opens a way out of the exclusive tribalism of the Yahwistic nation into potential universalism. This is the path taken most significantly by Paul, a pioneer. Yahweh is broadening his appeal and his claim: he now intends to become the Lord of all people and all the nations. In order to do this, however, it is necessary to displace his earlier chosen favorite – the people of Israel. A new people will become the people of the covenant. The new group is different from the old people of the covenant in that anyone can be adopted into the new group. It is no longer through exclusively blood and genetic line that one enters the community of chosen people, but it is now by the spirit that "blows where it wills, and you hear the sound of it, but you do not know whence it comes or whither it goes; so it is with everyone who is born of the Spirit."[47] The doors have been flung open and a free spirit is now in charge, not any longer the rulers of the chosen people.

The New Testament presents Jesus as heir to the mantle of special son and chosen one in numerous instances. One of the most provocative occurs in the story of Palm Sunday, when Jesus allows himself to be celebrated as king: "Hosanna! Blessed is he who comes in the name of the Lord! Blessed is the kingdom of our father David that is coming! Hosanna in the highest!"[48] Here Jesus is explicitly celebrated as the Messiah, just days before his crucifixion. But in more subtle ways, his teachings had earlier proven equally provocative.

---

[47] John 3:8.
[48] Mark 11:9-10.

In the parable of the Prodigal Son, for example, Jesus tells a story of reversal of privilege, which places the religious establishment, the priest and Pharisees, in a position of great discomfort and precisely names their emotional reaction to him: envy. It echoes the story of Cain and Abel, with the difference that the younger preferred son is not killed by his envious brother. Listen to the story, keeping in mind the stories of rivalrous brothers (Cain and Abel, Ishmael and Isaac, Jacob and Esau, and Joseph and his brothers) on the one hand, and the relations between Jesus and Israel on the other:

"There was a man who had two sons, and the younger of them said to his father, 'Father, give me the share of property that falls to me.' And he divided his living between them."[49]

Here the story is set up to portray the son asking and the father willingly giving him his inheritance; no trickery is involved. The son wants to leave home, and the father lets him. So the son goes off, wastes his money, and falls on hard times. Then he remembers his home, how comfortable it was, how his father had cared for him and loved him, and he says to himself: "I will arise and go to my father, and I will say.to him, 'Father, I have sinned against heaven and before you; I am no longer worthy to be called you son; treat me as one of your hired servants.'"[50]

This recognition of his waywardness is all well and good, he appears to be sincere, and when he comes home his father kills the fatted calf and celebrates his return. "Now his elder son was in the field, and as he came and drew near

---

[49] Luke 15:11-12.
[50] Luke 15:17-19.

to the house, he heard music and dancing. And he called one of the servants and asked what this meant. And he said to him, 'Your brother has come and our father has killed the fatted calf because he has received him safe and sound.' But he was angry and refused to go in. His father came out and entreated him, but he answered his father, 'Lo, these many years I have served you, and I never disobeyed your command; yet you never gave me a kid, that I might make merry with my friends. But when this son of yours came, who has devoured your living with harlots, you killed for him the fatted calf.'"[51]

Here is the envy reaction of the elder brother who senses his father's irrational emotional preference for the younger son. The father's attempt at soothing him couldn't have been very effective: "'Son, you are always with me, and all that is mine is yours. It was fitting to make merry and be glad, for this your brother was dead, and is alive; he was lost, and is found.'"[52] This story offers a penetrating insight into the psychological dynamics of the New Testament. Jesus, another son of Yahweh, suddenly appears on the scene and starts including elements of the population who had been religiously excluded, such as tax collectors, harlots, and Samaritans. These do not officially belong to the elect of God, to the chosen people. Yet now Jesus portrays the Father as embracing them enthusiastically. Where is the justice? Is this the reward earned for being good and obeying the law to the last letter?

God the Father is shown to prefer these wayward children in certain respects: for them He kills the fatted calf,

---

[51] Luke 15:25-30.
[52] Luke 15:31-32.

and for them there is rejoicing in heaven. Jesus' assertions about how God is reacting to the human scene, about what makes Him happy and pleased, and about whom He favors and whom He is willing to bless have been completely reversed from traditional teaching. In parables like this one and others (think, for instance, of the parable of the wicked tenants, in which the scribes and Pharisees are portrayed as servants and Jesus as the King's son), Jesus speaks of a profound change in Yahweh's attitude: no longer are the "chosen people" quite so special, in fact they are in danger of losing their heritage. For them, as for Cain, sin is crouching at the door, and if they succumb to the temptation to act out their envy they will suffer a fate similar to Cain's: banishment from their homeland and an identity of the eternal fugitive and wanderer who is persecuted wherever he happens to cross the path of others.

It was this Cain-like identity that was hung on the Jews by medieval Christian Europe and by Christendom generally until recently. For Israel did succumb to the temptation of envy and slew the innocent and favored son of Yahweh, according to the biblical narrative. The New Testament drama repeats the original fratricide enacted by Cain on Abel. In both cases the motivation was envy. It is not until our own day that anyone in a position of religious authority in either Judaism or Christendom could say with sincerity that both religions are sons of the same father, or that both belong to the same tradition. The history of the relations between Christians and Jews has been characterized by the dynamics evident already in the parable of the Prodigal Son and by the Cain and Abel motif: the elder envies and kills the younger son. Those who have identified with the younger son, the adopted children, have turned around and attacked the descendants of the elder son. The claim to supremacy of the younger over the older lies behind the signification of the Hebrew Scriptures as the "OLD Testament," and for those having to do with Jesus, the younger and now favored son, the "NEW Testament." Testament is synonymous with covenant: This is a new covenant. As Paul teaches in his letter to the Christians in Corinth concerning the Last Supper, repeating the words of Jesus as passed down to him: "This cup is the new covenant in my blood."[53] The old agreement between Yahweh and His chosen people was now declared null and void, or at least severely changed, as the throngs of adopted gentiles moved into the house of Israel and set up their spiritual homes there.

The thinkers of the New Testament struggled to find a way of accommodating the two sons, elder and younger, in the same household. But their effort failed, as it had to, since they could not, and did not, relinquish the claim of Jesus Christ's supremacy as Lord and of the new covenant over the old. The elder brother, Israel, could join in the new covenant if he desired, but to do so he must give up his claim of exclusive chosenness in favor of recognizing the lordship of Christ and the legitimacy of his new followers as children of God. Israel did not do this. Instead, he continued advancing his own claim to exclusivity and chosenness. The two brothers coexist now, occasionally in some measure of harmony and mutual understanding, but still often in a spirit of rivalry and suspicion that is loaded with shadow projection. Envy continues to crouch at the door.

Having noted the ubiquity and repetitiousness of the dynamic we are discussing – willing, choosing, and prefer-

---

[53] I Corinthians 11:25.

ring on the part of the Yahweh archetype, followed by rivalry, envy, and enmity between the factions discriminated – we are left with the question: What is the psychological meaning of this dynamic? A pattern that repeats itself so frequently in dreams must have a special meaning that consciousness is meant to "get." In the biblical dream, the Yahweh archetype is shown to be seeking incarnation, i.e., integration, at more conscious levels. As this archetype approaches consciousness, the effect of it is for the ego to prefer one set of traits over another – one line of development over the other possibilities – and in this way, it gradually creates a pattern in consciousness like itself. The archetype gradually structures consciousness. This produces an attitude in consciousness that resembles the pattern of the archetype. In moving toward consciousness in this fashion, the traits and developmental possibilities that do not fit in with the archetypal pattern become rejects and turn into shadow aspects of the developing conscious person. Thus, a tension is created between the conscious subject's identity and persona pattern on the one hand and a shadow personality on the other. In the biblical individuation story, this is a particularly sharp contrast because the archetype (Yahweh) is so insistent on having its way and no other. This dynamic insistence must be related to the overall individuation process.

Most probably, it was created by an equally, or almost equally, insistent dynamic in the opposite direction. That is to say, it is probably compensatory for an attitude that would deny it. If we look upon Yahweh as an animus figure, then the force denying Him His entry into consciousness would be the former prejudice against the animus in the Great Mother. In any case, we can safely assume that in order to make His appearance in consciousness, the Yahweh archetype had to overcome rather great forces of resistance and inertia, regressive forces, and that this accounts, in part at least, for His fierce insistence on having it His way: His law must be obeyed, there must be no other gods before Him, etc. And this, in turn, reproduced the strong discriminating tendency on the surface of the dream: this way not that, this one not that, etc.

By the time Yahweh becomes incarnated in Jesus, a clear line of development has been established. The people of Israel are solidly fixed in their ways. Jesus, in part, represents an attempt to take the development one step further, toward shadow and anima integration – "he who is without sin cast the first stone," wining and dining with the tax collector and harlots, go ye therefore into all the world, etc. – and there is a genuine attempt in the New Testament to break down the barriers created by the Yahwistic attitude in the Old Testament. But at the same time, the appearance of Jesus also creates a further division of the same sort, and a new kind of shadow brother emerges in the elder brother, Israel. Moreover, as St. Paul testifies, the old Adam and the new continue to exist in uneasy tension even within the Christian, so the shadow problem has clearly not been solved. If anything, the biblical individuation process as represented in the line of development shown in the biblical dream text instructs us that the inevitable price paid for a spiritually discriminating state of consciousness, that is, for this kind of development, is a sharp tension between the ideals of consciousness and the shadow. All who have tried to live by this book have had to struggle with the problem of the two rivalrous brothers, moral ego and immoral shadow.

From King to Servant – Ego Relativization

When I was a boy, my favorite biblical character was David. His daring and his heroism stirred my imagination, but probably also his sheer luck and gifts as a poet were a part of his appeal. I would often dwell on tense stories like the one about the time David tracked Saul down in his hideout in the mountains, found his cave, and while preparing to kill him, changed his mind and left a token behind to let Saul know what had happened when he awoke. David was a kid who could come from behind, who went up against giants, who always came out on top. In my mind, he was a lot like the Lone Ranger and other heroes. Only, he was better because he was more complex. The Lone Ranger didn't compose and sing songs, take care of melancholy kings, or become a king himself. David, besides being a hero in the warrior sense, is a cultural hero and also a religious hero. And his humanness stands out. He is much more likeable than many of the biblical figures are, and certainly as a young person I had an easier time identifying with him than with the ancient fathers or with Moses, let alone the prophets or with the New Testament figures like John the Baptist or Jesus or the heroes of the faith like Peter and Paul. The only figure who could come close to David for me was Joseph, and at the time I wasn't much into interpreting dreams. So David it was. It is true, however, that we did not dwell on the more gory and gruesome details of the David saga as recounted in the Books of Samuel. In later years, I have come to recognize him as a flawed and tragic figure as well, but still appealing for all of that.

David is about the closest we have in the biblical dream text to a realistic ego figure. His image is not particularly symbolic, even though he did the impossible in killing Goliath with a slingshot and filled an archetypal role as king. Nevertheless, he lived a credible human life. Born into a big country family, he grows up among a bunch of brothers; he acts the part of a hero for a time and then of a bandit and hunted outlaw; he wins the struggle with King Saul, becomes king and then falls into lustful temptation and commits the sins of murder (indirectly) and adultery. He pays for these sins with terrible guilt, but this also contributes to making him a great religious poet. In old age, he feels the cold and suffers sleeping in bed alone, so a pretty young girl by the name of Abishag is found to sleep with him and keep him warm. He dies of old age, somewhat troubled about the line of succession, while Bathsheba schemes to have her son, Solomon, installed after David. This is a normal-sounding life, even if it is quite illustrious and special. It is important to note that he is much favored by Yahweh. He is chosen by Yahweh to replace Saul with whom Yahweh is disappointed. David is therefore a further incarnation of the Yahweh archetype, now in the form of an accomplished and suffering ego.

This normality shown in the figure of David is, psychologically speaking, a great achievement and marks an advance in the individuation process that is depicted in the biblical dream narrative. If we take into account the biblical dream text as a whole, David symbolizes a stage of psychological development achieved. This is the stage of ego consolidation, the fulfillment of individuation in the first half of life. David is the first member of the Israelite people to become an effective and successful king. His immediate predecessor, Saul, is chronologically the first king of Israel, but he represents a pre-ego-consolidation stage and ends in failure. Saul is named king reluctantly by the prophet Samuel and does function as king, but he is an unsteady personality and mostly serves to break the ground for his successor, King David, the one who in the biblical dream is shown as the model figure of the resilient and stable ego.

In the Bible, King David is the ultimate king, never to be surpassed. And this is why Jesus' connection to David is so important for defining his later meaning. Because he is of the lineage of David, it means that Jesus stands in close relation to the king archetype. This juxtaposition of Jesus and David, both kingly figures, will highlight one of the central symbolic meanings of Jesus' existence.

The appearance of such a king as David in this dream text, the Bible, signifies a stage of individuation achieved within the context of the narrative as a whole. If we take the Bible as the account of an individuation process, we can mark certain stages and high points within its overall arc. There is the beginning, when Yahweh appears and creates order out of chaos, giving birth to consciousness. This is followed by the primal pair in the garden, an image for early and mostly pre-conscious wholeness, the paradisal state of unity with the parent figure and the surrounding world. Consciousness then increases through the suffering inflicted as a result of disobedience and the expulsion from the paradisal garden. This separation from the womb and the mother's nurturing embrace marks the entry into egohood, the sense of reality as the ego knows it. With it, comes the division between ego-persona and shadow (Abel and Cain) along with a stark division of labor and identity between the sexes. There follows an extended period of lethal threat and conflict (the flood, threats of annihilation and abandonment). This turbulent period comes to an end, or rather, is taken up into the next phase of development when Moses receives the Law and forges the covenantal agreement between the tribes of Israel and Yahweh at Shechem. The achievement of ego-consciousness, which Freud would speak of as the resolution of the Oedipal complex, leaves this personality with a clear character structure and the beginnings of a definite identity based on adherence to the Mosaic code and the legal system that evolved from it. At the death of Moses, the people are complete in a certain sense, and the first five books of the Bible, traditionally known as the Books of Moses, comprise the heart of the Hebrew Scriptures, the Torah. This is the basis of this people's identity throughout the rest of the story.

By this point, Yahweh can be somewhat satisfied with his work. He has forged a people and has set them well on their way to defining their tribe in His image. This will be Yahweh's means for incarnating in history. As Moses watches from the hills overlooking the Jordan river, the people take their leave of him and follow Joshua off into the conquest of the promised land. They face a large and powerful enemy, and their courage and faith will be tested to the limit as they invade this territory. But they have confidence that the Lord is on their side and is leading them, as He did in the wilderness during their flight from Egypt. This is a confederation of families that stem from a common ancestor that is being guided by the mysterious hidden hand of Yahweh. They have no designated king. They have a series of leaders (the

"Judges") who are directly inspired and instructed by Yahweh to take prisoners or not, when and where to engage in combat or not, and to worship at certain places or to avoid them as unclean. This is a personality, then, without a clearly established ego function. It is scattered, vague and operating on intuition, taking its cues from the unconscious and the hints of ancestral voices. Since this people has its mission clearly marked out for it – to take the land and to settle it – there is not much need for further leadership. This is a kind of idealized period in Israel's history, not without failures and flaws but in retrospect seen as a time when Israel was especially close to Yahweh. Yahweh was the military general and the political leader, and the Judges simply passed along His words and intentions.

On the ground, the twelve tribes make up a rather loosely organized confederation with minimal central authority. They get together to fight or to worship, but in matters of governance and administration, they are quite independent and separate. In developmental terms, this is a loosely knit personality of autonomous complexes that work together in harmony enough of the time to be adaptive and to survive the challenges of the environment. It is a sort of latency period, developmentally speaking. The judges seem to have special access to Yahweh, like the prophets after them, and this openness is pleasing to Yahweh, who acts as a parental superego. This is a personality at a stage of development that is governed by archetypal powers and intuition more than by a conscious will (ego). The Judges are, for the most part, attractive and estimable figures, deeply religious, and committed to the directions given by Yahweh. This is the theocratic period in Israel's history.

The last of the Judges is Samuel, who is also arguably the greatest, but when it comes time for Samuel to pass the mantel on, he makes the mistake of designating his own sons as the next generation of Judges, and they turn out to be corrupt. They cheat the people and try to get rich from their position of privilege. So the people use this as an excuse to demand a king. The elders come to him and say, "Behold, you are old and your sons do not walk in your ways; now appoint for us a king to govern us like all the nations."[54]

They could have asked for another Judge to be designated if they didn't like Samuel's sons, but instead they ask for a king in order to be like all the other nations. This is what teenagers typically ask for and do: all the others have one, we want one too! It is a stage of self-assertion and peer pressure to conform. The psyche is demanding a new stage in its configuration. But for this personality, it is a dangerous step forward, for this people is, precisely, different from all the others. It has to be different in order to incarnate the creative archetype Yahweh, for Yahweh is different from the gods of the other peoples. He demands an exclusive position. This is the inauguration of monotheism, a radical centralization of authority in one figure. The other people have pantheons, goddesses, Baals, and they eat pigs and other unclean animals (mice, even); moreover, they do not have the Law, they do not have this special history, they do not have the covenant. So it is dangerous to start thinking of oneself too much as being like the others. One falls into danger of forgetting the ways in which one is essentially NOT like the others if one becomes too much like them. Having a king comes dangerously close to losing this special

---

[54] 1 Samuel 8:4.

difference and therefore to losing touch with the archetype that has created this identity. Yahweh is upset, and so is Samuel.

Samuel prays to the Lord and hears the Lord say to him: "Hearken to the voice of the people in all that they say to you; for they have not rejected you, but they have rejected me from being king over them. According to all the deeds which they have done to me, from the day I brought them up out of Egypt even to this day, forsaking me and serving other gods, so they are also doing to you. Now then, hearken to their voice; only, you shall solemnly warn them, and show them the ways of the king who shall reign over them."[55]

Asking for a king is seen by Yahweh as rejection of Him, not of Samuel. The king's authority will replace Yahweh's: the ego will replace the archetype as prime mover in this psyche. (This was Freud's dream when he declared, "Where id was, ego shall be!") Now the people will have a king and listen to him instead of listening to Yahweh, and they will become even more disobedient and alienated than they have been all along. Kingship spells distance from Yahweh. And yet, Yahweh goes along with it. He instructs Samuel in the means for selecting and anointing a king; He himself chooses Saul to be the first king; He arranges the whole affair. Though it is bitter for Yahweh to do so, He relinquishes the role of king and gives it over to the manic-depressive figure, Saul. Now there will be a greater distance between Yahweh and His people.

When the ego becomes kinglike and enters this phase of its role in the development of the personality, access and openness to the unconscious diminishes. From now on it will be more difficult to set up lines of communication between

---

[55] 1 Samuel 7:9.

THE BIBLE AS DREAM

the archetypal level of Yahweh and the conscious level of the human psyche. It will be left to the intuitives – the Prophets – to keep this line of communication open as much as they can. The relations between prophets and kings were ever uneasy. The king sets his goals and makes his decisions based on conscious and so-called rational considerations, while the prophet listens to the archetypal psyche, in this case to Yahweh. The king is the pragmatic ego; the prophet represents the uncompromising voice of the archetype. While the ego seeks compromise and short-term advantage, the archetype insists on absolutes and ultimate fulfillment of its emergent momentum toward incarnation.

This conflict leads to Saul's demise as king. Saul is told by Samuel, who speaks for Yahweh, to go up against the Amalekites and to destroy them utterly: "Thus says the Lord of hosts, 'I will punish what Amalek did to Israel in opposing them on the way, when they came up out of Egypt. Now go and smite Amalek, and utterly destroy all that they have; do not spare them, but kill both man and woman, infant and suckling, ox and sheep, camel and ass.'"[56]

The motive here is revenge for what the Amalekites did to the chosen people earlier. For that they are to be destroyed. Saul has his own views on the matter, however, and does not heed Samuel's instructions. He spares some of the Amalekites, the Kenites, who have shown the Israelites some kindness; he does not kill King Agag; and he saves the livestock captured, destroying only the despised and worthless things. From a practical point of view, i.e., the ego's viewpoint, this was sensible. But from Yahweh's viewpoint, it is high treason. "I repent that I have made Saul

---

[56] 1 Samuel 15:3.

king; for he has turned back from following me; and has not performed my commandments."[57] And so Samuel confronts Saul: "You have rejected the word of the Lord, and the Lord has also rejected you from being king over Israel."[58] Saul, in turn, tries to reason with Samuel, but Samuel will have none of it. In fact, he takes matters into his own hands: "Then Samuel said, 'Bring here to me Agag the king of the Amalekites.' And Agag came to him cheerfully. Agag said, 'Surely the bitterness of death is past.' And Samuel said, 'As your sword has made women childless, so shall your mother be childless among women.' And Samuel hewed Agag in pieces before the Lord in Gilgal."[59] After Agag receives his deserts, Samuel repudiates Saul and goes off to find his successor. But he grieves over Saul even while "the Lord repented that he had made Saul king over Israel."[60] Yahweh is hard and unforgiving.

On instructions from Yahweh, then, who says to Samuel: "How long will you grieve over Saul, seeing I have rejected him from being king over Israel? Fill your horn with oil, and go; I will send you to Jesse the Bethlehemite, for I have provided for myself a king among his sons,"[61] the faithful Judge makes his way to Bethlehem and asks Jesse to see his sons. One by one, they pass before him in review, but none receives the blessing from Yahweh needed to declare him king. After seeing seven sons pass before him, all of them rejected by Yahweh, Samuel asks if he has seen them all, and Jesse admits there is one more, the youngest, who is out

---

keeping the sheep. When he comes in, the text says that "he was ruddy, and had beautiful eyes, and was handsome. And the Lord said, 'Arise, anoint him; for this is he.'"[62] Samuel anoints David "with the horn of oil, and anointed him in the midst of his brothers; and the Spirit of the Lord came mightily upon David from that day forward."[63]

Thus, David becomes the anointed one, the king of Israel, but it is still a long while before he can claim his kingdom. Through iconography and symbolic representation, Saul later becomes a figure of the old king, Saturn, melancholic, and a senex. This is the old attitude that has outlived its usefulness, yet hangs on for dear life. It is an ego attitude that will not die easily, even though it is no longer supported by deeper levels of the personality. Saul comes to represent the resistance to change and transformation on the part of an outmoded ego attitude. David, on the contrary, represents the upstart *puer aeternus* full of himself, brimming with confidence, tricksterish, and blessed with good fortune.

Synchronicity smiles on him. Everything he tries comes out right. He is immensely gifted in spirit and has precisely the zest and sparkle lacking in the old king. Naturally, the old king becomes envious of him and tries to kill him. Again, envy crouches at the door and springs into action because the favoritism of Yahweh has passed to another. David is the golden boy, the younger favorite son, and thus in line with such notables as Jacob and Joseph. It is his destiny to become king of Israel.

The kingship of David is a great success. Unlike the rule of Saul, his predecessor, David's role as king does not collapse

---

[62] 1 Samuel 16:12.
[63] 1 Samuel 16:13.

in misfortune. David is able to unite the twelve tribes under one ruler, establish Jerusalem as the capitol of the country, and able to lay the foundations for the centralized government that will grow and reach its zenith of prosperity and magnificence under his son, Solomon. But in this very success are also the seeds of destruction, for as a result of this secular achievement, the kingdom gradually grows corrupt, eventually fragments, and ultimately disintegrates into factions and loses its way. Then, the kingdom is conquered by neighbors and the inhabitants of the land are taken captive to Babylon. In David and his rulership, we see a truly successful ego development reaching its culmination. David is practical and disciplined enough to conquer and govern, and he retains a sense of Yahweh's presence and His pleasure or displeasure. He shows a fine balance between an ego orientation to the reality of practical affairs and adaptation to outer concerns on the one side, and an orientation to the anima and the inner world of dreams, inspired thoughts, imagination, and conscience on the other. As the people celebrate him and his victories, he in turn celebrates the Lord and thus keeps some perspective on his place within the greater order, for the great danger of kingship is inflation.

Ego inflation occurs when the ego gets itself confused with the archetypal backing that supports its position. When this occurs the ego loses its inner and outer balance. On the outer level, it cannot any longer make sound reality judgments, and it overreaches itself. On the inner level, the same thing happens: the religious attitude is lost, and the ego's will becomes all. "If I think it, it must be true," is the way this kind of a kingly ego behaves. The results are inevitable, and only a matter of time must pass until disaster strikes. This is why Yahweh was so leery of the institution of kingship. With a king, this people will become inflated and think it can do whatever it pleases. It will lose touch with the bigger picture of history. It will forget its mission and why it became a special people in the first place. It will lose its identity as a chosen people "holy unto the Lord."

And yet, it was necessary for Israel to experience kingship. It is an important stage of individuation and forms the climax of personality development in the first half of life. Why is it necessary? Why must we have an ego like this? Need we become kings and have a kingdom of our own? Need we take possession of the land and put aside our dependence on all those who helped us and gave us the direction and mission and resources to get there? From a psychological viewpoint, it is not necessary to go through this fierce heroic stage in order to become a fully functioning person, but it is necessary if that person is going to embody an archetype and thereby bring something new into his or her previous culture.

One can achieve an identity through persona development, but it is an outer directed one and will be an identity based on the collective consensus. The creative individual follows a more risky path by attending to an inner sense of vocation. Incarnating an archetype is a ferocious undertaking full of extremes that reflect the opposites within the archetype. Had Yahweh settled for Saul and his accommodations to his neighbors, one can surmise that the Israelites would have quickly melted into the surrounding populations. Yahweh must be uncompromising in order to maintain His unique identity among the competing influences. This heroic period of conquest and warfare, led by fierce warrior types such as Deborah and Samuel and culminating in the tough guerrilla fighter, David, was the prerequisite for establishing this particular personality on the plane of history. This would be an identity based not on persona accommodations to the surrounding culture, but on a new archetype, an inner voice that could be heard only by some sensitive individuals in the stillness of the desert. As murder in dreams represents repression, so Samuel's vicious act of hacking King Agag to pieces, and his unrelenting conquest of the peoples who inhabited the promised land represents the structuring of this personality through a strong tendency toward repression. The purpose of this repression was to strengthen the tie between Yahweh, the archetype, and His chosen people. In this way, the kingship of figures such as David stood a chance of maintaining a connection with the archetype, Yahweh, despite the strong competing claims set up by the ego's natural orientation to outer reality and the surrounding cultural values.

The danger of having a centralized ego, a king, is twofold: it can become inflated by identifying with the archetype and thereby trying to swallow the archetype, so to speak, in its own sense of god-almightiness, or it can lose the sense of uniqueness and special mission in the world through accommodation to the environment, to "reality." Forever the Hebrews have walked this thin line between inflation as the chosen people and loss of identity through assimilation. It is a central individuation dilemma that has no easy formulaic solution.

With David, Israel begins a new phase of its in-dividuation history. A kingdom is established, the tribes are united, and a consolidated personality is achieved. There is now a cultic center in Jerusalem, which will become the site of the temple, and a priesthood and a court become established side by side. The king represents secular authority

– the ego – and the priesthood functions to remind the people of its deeper identity and its sacred history and to keep it in touch with its archetypal background. This project of consolidation is brought to its peak during the reign of David's wise son, Solomon. Its zenith is celebrated when the Queen of Sheba pays a visit to Jerusalem. She was the queen of the Sabeans, a people located in the part of the Arabian Peninsula that is today the country of Yemen, who were ruled by queens at the time (the 8th century BCE). She hears of Solomon's wisdom and wealth and comes to see for herself. What she sees surpasses even the grandest reports she had received beforehand:

"The report was true which I heard in my own land of your affairs and of your wisdom, but I did not believe the reports until I came and my own eyes had seen it; and, behold, the half was not told me; your wisdom and prosperity surpass the report which I heard. Happy are your wives! Happy are these your servants, who continually stand before you and hear your wisdom! Blessed be the Lord your God, who has delighted in you and set you on the throne of Israel! Because the Lord loved Israel forever, he has made you king, that you may execute justice and righteousness."[64]

This is the apotheosis of kingship: wisdom and wealth, recognition from the neighboring peoples, impressive monuments and buildings, and a secure kingdom that supposedly reflects the values of the archetype, Yahweh. But no sooner is it achieved than corruption begins to set in. Solomon, for all his wisdom, has a weakness, and it is for foreign women: "Now King Solomon loved many foreign women" and "clung to these in love": "He had seven hundred wives, princesses,

---

[64] 1 Kings 10:6-9.

and three hundred concubines; and his wives turned away his heart. For when Solomon was old, his wives turned away his heart after other gods; and his heart was not wholly true to the Lord his God, as was the heart of David his father."[65]

In his folly he builds altars to various other deities, among them Ashtoreth, the goddess of the Sidonians. Solomon seems to have had at least two motives in taking all these wives and concubines: political and amorous. According to the text, he loved these foreign women, and according to scholars, his probable motive was alliance from the neighbors.

Either way, it was seen by Yahweh and the dreaming consciousness to be an abandonment of the covenant with Yahweh and therefore represented a threat to the people's integrity. The ego, so arduously established through heroic effort and repression, again loses its way in accommodation to outer (political) reality concerns, and in attraction to other archetypal possibilities – the goddesses, the anima seduction. Yahweh is determined that His people reflect and embody *HIM* and not the other available archetypes. After Solomon, the experiment of kingship continues through several generations, but increasingly, the kingdom falls into fragments. The kings are weak and ineffectual, and the nation divides into northern and southern portions following ancient tribal divisions. Then these two kingdoms, Israel to the north and Judah to the south, are conquered by invading armies of neighboring powers and their peoples taken into exile.

Throughout, Yahweh is shown to be more or less disgusted with His people: with their rivalry and jealousies,

---

[65] I Kings 11:1-4.

.

145

their impulsiveness and greed, and their carelessness about following the spirit and the letter of His law. Much of this history of fragmentation and dismemberment is seen, in the biblical dream account, as Yahweh's punishment for disobedience and waywardness. Because this people does not listen and obey, but follows its own wanton proclivity, it is allowed to fall to pieces. In all of this, we witness an extremely troubled phase of this individuation process. In an individual person's life, this would look like a prolonged midlife crisis, beginning after a strong consolidation of the ego position and securing of an inner and outer kingdom.

Here the pieces of consciousness fall asunder; conflicting impulses tear the fabric that had been woven; and there is a general breakdown both in the persona (the kingdom is taken captive and lost from the face of history as a nation) and in the deeper centers of ego identity. This is a crisis of massive proportions that shakes the people's confidence in its specialness and its vocation to be Yahweh's chosen people of the covenant. It is during this period of upheaval and confusion that the voice of the prophet comes forth. It is the prophetic voice of this liminal period that expresses this people's religious genius and sets the stage for the next phase of individuation as told in the story of Jesus of Nazareth.

If the first half of life culminates in kingship, the second emphasizes the figure of the suffering servant. The essential lesson left by the first phase of Biblical individuation was the supremacy of the covenant and the law over later ego development. From a Freudian perspective, one would see this as the product of the Oedipal complex, whereby the father remains superior to the son, and the superego (which is the deposit of the father and his law) over the ego. From the point of view put forward earlier that the Bible can be read as the story of animus development, this outcome can be read as the victory of the archetypal animus over the husband figure (the king). From a Jungian theoretical position, one would take it as the conclusion of the first half of life of ego development and the beginning of the second half, in which the ego position is relativized in favor of a larger sense of the self. It cannot be denied that the essential deposit left by the early Yahwistic period is the supremacy of law over personality. This is also the bedrock of value upon which western democracy rests, and without it our system of pluralism would be impossible. The law will eventually become a container that can hold together the competing claims of millions of individual egos without fragmenting the whole into as many splinters as there are strong-willed individuals.

In order for our sense of the supremacy of law over individual preference and charismatic leader to actually become effective and make a pluralistic society possible, however, there must also be the notion of an evolving system of laws (the "common law" idea) that, through a process of interpretation and expanding reflection, can accommodate new developments. The inability to accommodate new developments creates a Procrustean bed into which society and the individual must fit, which results in rigid legalism. This sterile outcome of individuation, represented by the legalistic attitude of senex consciousness, is what the prophets seek to avoid. They are the earliest creative interpreters of the law and of Yahweh's will. It was out of this profound need to keep individuation alive to new creative possibilities while preserving the spirit of the covenant and the essence of Yahweh that a new attitude was proposed for ego-consciousness. A new ego ideal evolved. Rather than the "king," which represents Yahweh in his archetypal power and awesome authority, the "servant" was proposed, which would represent another side of the Yahweh archetype: its concern for integration of various shunned elements.

If the king is established by division, repression, and differentiation, the servant is established by integration and accommodation. The purpose of the first movement is identity; the goal of the second is integrated selfhood. The second Isaiah proposes the image of the suffering servant in four passages. There has been much scholarly debate about who this is supposed to represent. Is it an individual? The people of Israel as a whole? A group within the nation of Israel? The point of reference is extremely unclear. Who is speaking, and who are they speaking about?

"Who has believed what we have heard? And to whom has the arm of the Lord been revealed? For he grew up before him like a young plant, and like a root out of dry ground; he had no form or comeliness that we should look at him, and no beauty that we should desire him. He was despised and rejected by men; a man of sorrows, and acquainted with grief; and as one from whom men hide their faces he was despised, and we esteemed him not.

"Surely he has borne our griefs and carried our sorrows; yet we esteemed him stricken, smitten by God, and afflicted. But he was wounded for our transgressions, he was bruised for our iniquities; upon him was the chastisement that made us whole, and with his stripes we are healed. All we, like sheep, have gone astray; we have turned everyone to his own way. And the Lord has laid on him the iniquity of us all."

It is this servant figure whom Yahweh approves of and ultimately rewards. More than that, it is because of this figure that He rewards His people Israel. Because this is a symbol from the unconscious, it is ambiguous and overdetermined: it can be the few just persons who recognize the meaning of suffering; it could be a single individual; it could be a large group. These are unimportant details. The point is that Yahweh looks with favor on this attitude of consciously accepted suffering. The ego that once would have been king has now been ground down by adversity and tragedy, and instead of seeking to avoid the brunt of the suffering by looking for routes of escape or various defenses (denial, adaptation and assimilation, violent aggression), this attitude accepts the suffering and bears the consequences for the earlier inflation and hubris. And it is because this attitude has come into being in consciousness somewhere that the whole people will be saved and blessed: they will be given back their land and they will prosper. But even beyond the restoration of Israel, the servant has a mission to extend the light of Yahweh's law to all the nations:

"It is too light a thing that you should be my servant to raise up the tribes of Jacob and to restore the preserved of Israel; I will give you as a light to the nations, that my salvation may reach to the end of the earth."[66]

It is this movement beyond the boundaries of Israel, beyond this unique identity, that sets the servant's role apart from that of the king. The king consolidates the people and leads it into a unity; the servant reaches out to the others, ignoring his own personal needs and desires.

This is certainly not to say that Yahweh is saying here that He is abandoning Israel in favor of the others, but that

---

[66] Isaiah 49:6.

both Israel and the others are to be included in the new, promised arrangement. The servant is the means by which this is supposed to be accomplished.

This is a somewhat surprising element in Yahweh's attitude toward mankind. Until this point in the story, He has been pretty much exclusively concerned with His own chosen people. The "others" have been seen as threats, obstacles, seducers, and have generally come in for a tough time of it if they happened to cross Yahweh's purposeful path. Now He begins to speak about including them in His purposes. They are to have light too. Yahweh himself is changing, and the new image, the servant, represents this new aspect of Yahweh manifesting itself.

The image of Yahweh's servant who suffers without complaint and through his acceptance of suffering is able to bring redemption not only to the dispossessed people of Israel but also to the other nations became a prime ingredient in the notion of a Messiah who was to come and save the people. The notion that the Messiah would come in the image of a suffering servant was not a new one when it came to the fore in the accounts of Jesus' life and death. As the Biblical text presents the story, Jesus consciously chose the role of suffering servant in his identity as Messiah and savior. He did this in order to fulfill the prophecies of the Scriptures. This was certainly a central part of the myth Jesus enacted. This myth was most crucially played out in The Passion, in the scenes created and the words spoken during the final weeks and days of Jesus' life. If there is room for doubt about who the suffering servant is in the book of Isaiah, there is none about who he is in the New Testament. He is this specific human being, Jesus of Nazareth.

Many passages from the New Testament writings could be adduced to show how Jesus was seen and saw himself in the role of suffering servant. One of the most dramatic and vivid occurs in the fourth Gospel when Jesus, during the Passover feast just before his being taken by the Roman soldiers, washes the feet of his disciples. Here he enacts the humble role of servant and in doing so attempts to teach his followers an important lesson. In this rather long passage in the Gospel of John, which extends from chapter 13 through 17, Jesus is shown as teaching his disciples about his identity, engaging them in the purpose of his ministry, and foretelling their future and that of the church after he leaves them. In this context, the first thing he does is wash their feet. They resist at first, until he explains what he is doing. Then he teaches them what this act means: "When he had washed their feet, and taken his garments, and resumed his place, he said to them, 'Do you know what I have done to you? You call me Teacher and Lord; and you are right, for so I am. If I then, your Lord and Teacher, have washed your feet, you also ought to wash one another's feet. For I have given you an example, that you also should do as I have done to you. Truly, truly, I say to you, a servant is not greater than his master; nor is he who is sent greater than he who sent him.'"[67] The message is quite clear, at least on one level: Jesus takes the role of servant, and so his disciples, who are not greater than he, should do the same. He is setting up a new ego ideal: do not strive to be king, to sit at the head of the table, or to be first; rather, serve others, take the last seat, take on the role of servants, not masters.

---

[67] John 13:12-16.

In the context of his teaching, however, there is a further meaning. For Jesus claims that he is sent by the Father, and he, in turn, is sending the disciples forth as the Father has sent him. He, as the one sent by the Father, cannot be greater than the one who sent him. Therefore, he must accept the role of the servant. The implication is that the Father also is taking the role of servant, and that this is being passed on down the chain of command: as the Father is a servant, so the son whom He sends is to be a servant, so the disciples whom the son sends forth are to be servants. In playing the role of servant, he is expressing an aspect of the Father's identity. He is showing Yahweh as servant rather than as master. Not that the sense of chain of command and hierarchy is undermined; it is not. Rather, Yahweh puts forward a new ego ideal, emphasizing that the proper way to mirror Him and to incarnate Him in ego-consciousness is to become servant-like.

It is not uncommon to say that archetypes contain polarities and that as they seek to enter consciousness they tend to divide or split. The task of consciousness becomes to try to hold the tension of the opposites so that the archetype can be integrated more or less wholly into consciousness. In the image of Jesus, we see this polarity within the Yahweh archetype. On the one hand he is king, ruler, and lord; on the other he is servant. What is being offered is a healer vocation: by themselves becoming seriously ill patients and finding the healing substance within themselves they will be able to offer it to others who are ill. The suffering servant is such a figure. "By his stripes we are healed" is the telling sign. Because he takes on the sickness of the people who need healing, he can eventually produce, from his own willing and conscious suffering, the medicine that will heal the others.

Thus, the suffering servant must be looked upon as a spiritual healer who has obtained the power to heal by virtue of his acceptance of suffering and by the consequent constellation of spiritual "medicine." This notion is graphically enacted in the ritual of the last supper, and later, in the ritual of holy communion: "this is my body, this is my blood" is the medicine generated by Jesus' suffering for the salvation of many.

As Jesus' role came to be understood in the New Testament, his identity as the suffering servant who can heal others and redeem the Israelites as well as all the other nations became central. He was the Messianic figure who had been promised by Isaiah. Added to this notion was the view that Jesus represented Yahweh directly and without distortion: "I and the Father are one!" was Christ reconciling the world to himself. In this image of Yahweh himself as suffering servant, we are exposed to His shamanic side, to His identification with the plight of the guilty and broken ego-consciousness of His children. In this aspect of His personality, Yahweh shows some maternal features. In the Messianic age, Isaiah prophesies, Yahweh will transform the earth: "For behold, I create new heavens and a new earth; and the former things shall not be remembered or come into mind. There will be feasting and rejoicing: Rejoice with Jerusalem, and be glad for her, all you who love her; rejoice with her in joy, all you who mourn over her; that you may suck and be satisfied with her consoling breasts; that you may drink deeply with delight from the abundance of her glory. For thus says the Lord: 'Behold, I will extend prosperity to her like a river, and the wealth of the nations like an over-flowing stream; and you shall suck, you shall be carried upon her hip, and dandled upon her knees. As one whom his mother comforts, so I will comfort you.'"[68]

Jesus later picks up this maternal image in his lament over Jerusalem, when, speaking for Yahweh, he cries: "O Jerusalem, Jerusalem, killing the prophets and stoning those who are sent to you! How often would I have gathered your children together as a hen gathers her brood under wings, and you would not!"[69]

This maternal attitude on God's part, which leads directly to the notion that God is love and is self-sacrificing for His children, could lead us to ask whether, psychologically speaking, another archetype other than the Yahwistic paternal one is making its appearance. Perhaps a second archetype, a maternal one, is inching its way toward consciousness and displacing the paternalistic Yahweh. This question, on a theological level, led some early thinkers to claim that the God of the New Testament is a fundamentally different God from that of the Old Testament. According to some Gnostic speculators, the Old Testament God was to be identified with the demiurge, a false god and creator of a bad universe, and the New Testament God was the true god and the redeemer of the soul from this corrupt system into which we have fallen. However, the tradition of holding the two testaments together prevailed, and the God of the Old Testament was seen as continuous with that of the New Testament. So if we take it this way, psychologically, we'd say that in the image of the suffering servant Yahweh is showing another side from the one revealed in His earlier images as creator and king of the universe.

---

[68] Isaiah 66:10-13.
[69] Matthew 23:37.

We are to hold these two poles of the same archetype in tension, but we are also seeing the movement from Old Testament to New Testament – from the creator/king image of the archetype to the suffering servant image – as a developmental sequence, so it's not merely that the first side of the archetype shows and then the other, but that in the movement of this archetype into consciousness, the earlier impact upon ego-consciousness leads to an identity as king – an ego state that sees itself as in control of its destiny and with maximal authority in its own right – to an identity as servant. But, in assuming this new identity, the old identity as king is still included, only now in a symbolic and "psychological" rather than literal way.

Jesus is shown repeatedly as king. He has a kingdom, he wears a crown, he rides into Jerusalem in triumph, and he is named the King of the Jews, but this identity as king is presented in the spiritual sense. "My kingdom is not of this world." The parables of the kingdom tell about a state of mind not a secular state of buildings and bureaus. He has disciples, not soldiers, and yet they want to sit at his right hand when he comes into his kingdom, and he has to disabuse them. Jesus takes the identity of king but also undercuts it, deconstructs it, and psychologizes it. It is with grim irony that that he allows himself to be crowned and named King of the Jews. In taking this identity upon himself, he also destroys it, grinds it to powder, and relativizes it. It is decisively subsumed under his identity as suffering servant.

Now, in this kingdom, the last shall be first and the first last; the king shall be servant, and the servant shall be king; the beggar Lazarus will rest in the bosom of Abraham while the miserly king who turned him away will cry for a drop of water. This will fulfill the words of the prophet Isaiah:

"Therefore, thus says the Lord God: 'Behold, my servants shall eat, but you shall be hungry; behold, my servants shall drink, but you shall be thirsty; behold, my servants shall rejoice, but you shall be put to shame. But this is the man to whom I will look, he that is humble and contrite in spirit, and trembles at my word.'"[70]

Or, in the words of Jesus: "Blessed are the poor in spirit, for theirs is the kingdom of heaven."[71]

There is a deep point of agreement between the Old and New Testaments, both Hebrew and Christian Scriptures, on the goal of individuation resulting in the human identity of servanthood. We could call this by the Ericsonian name of generativity, which Erik Erikson designates as the prime task in the period following identity consolidation and the achievement of intimacy as a lived value. The New Testament perhaps takes it a step further in asserting that Yahweh Himself takes the form of a servant through the incarnation of Himself as His son in Jesus Christ. In Christ, God set the example of how it is to be done, and in doing it Himself, also revealed His essence to be love. Christians would not assert that love replaces justice or abrogates it ("justice" having been the earlier prime value revealed through the law), but that it completes and fulfills it. The product of this individuation process is a consciousness that rests on the twin values of justice and love, but the greater of these is love.

Jung's critique of the biblical tradition does not aim to undermine it, but to encourage its movement to a still further step of wholeness. Both Old and New Testaments culminate in a promise of a new heaven and new earth. Isaiah

---

[70] Isaiah 65:13; 66:2.
[71] Matthew 5:3.

and Revelation are companion volumes in this sense and should be read side by side. Revelation depicts wholeness and completion in two great images: the marriage of the lamb and the new Jerusalem. The coniunctio image of the lamb marrying his bride symbolizes the union in heaven of heaven and earth. The new Jerusalem, a perfect cube with streets of transparent gold and every imaginable jewel in its doors and foundations, is a perfect symbol of psychological wholeness realized. The problem is that they remain at the level of ideals, projections, and therefore still in the unconscious. What has been produced so far in this individuation process that the biblical text depicts is what the alchemists called the *unio mentalis*: the extraction of the soul from matter and its union with the spirit. This is the first stage of consciousness-making. It is the level of dream, image, insight, and intuition. What comes next is the union of this product with the rejected body lying inert in the bottom of the flask. This is the second union, which represents the movement from idea and ideal into reality – from unconscious to consciousness as lived experience. Jung speaks of this as the problem of the three and the four: the three represents ideals, and the four represents full-bodied reality. The difficulty of traversing this space is enormous.

Certainly the history of Judaism and Christianity is filled with individuals who have tried mightily to live concretely by the ideals expressed in the text. This is the *imitatio Christi* as traditionally understood. The suffering servant image is expressed in the Jewish teaching of the ten just men, for example, and in contemporary Jewish thinking the Holocaust is sometimes seen as the manifestation of the suffering servant in history, the chosen people as suffering in preparation for the return of Israel as a Jewish nation. In

Christian history, such figures as St. Francis and many of the other saints are exemplary of the lived ideal of the suffering servant. The kingly ego is crushed and subsumed under the identity of the servant role. There are numerous instances of such attempts to fully embody the values of justice and love. As institutions go, the church has fallen woefully short, obviously, and has often been successfully tempted to putting on the kingly robes and taking up the scepter of power and secular wealth, losing its sense of the role of suffering servant to man-king. Yet, the ideals have always called it back to that path and continue to do so even today.

As Jung looked at history, however, he saw that the tradition had achieved a great deal in the way of psychological development and consciousness, but still had a ways to go. In a sense, it was running out of steam, and the symbols that had sustained its spiritual life were failing as science, the modern religion, and other political myths were crowding the cultural scene and making the Judeo-Christian myth look more and more unrealistic and irrelevant. It needed a new boost, a fresh impetus for the next leg of its development. But beyond this, it needed to take the next necessary step in individuation, which was to attempt making the connection between ideals and "body" in a new way.

What had been left behind and neglected and continued to be problematic, despite the best conscious efforts of believers, were the body (the feminine, as he spoke of it symbolically) and the shadow. These had been dealt with in the tradition largely through denial: denial of the flesh on the one side, and denial of the reality of evil in the doctrine of *privatio boni* on the other. This leaves religious doctrine too up in the air – too much in the realm of ideals and ego power: I will try to be better, more spiritual, more ideal.

Jung's approach was to make the attempt at integration in a different way. Rather than through conscious effort, meditation on the images of the Bible, spiritual exercises, prayer, cultic activities, etc., he recommended dealing with the unconscious and individuating in a personal way. Rather than trying to be more Christ-like in the traditional sense, his way was to become more self-like in a personal way. In this personal and individual approach, he felt, the task of carrying the tradition into the next stage would take place. It would be the individual, working diligently on himself or herself, honestly and sacrificially, bending the kingly ego to the servant's task of tending the psyche and nurturing its gradual development, who would eventually ground the wholeness promised in Isaiah and Revelation. The kingdom of God would come to earth through the inner work of the individual and through increasing consciousness and acceptance of the whole person as this is revealed through a personal individuation journey. It was only by breaking out of the mesmerizing grip of the collective individuation pathway presented by the great religious tradition of our heritage that the goal of individuation promised by that very heritage could actually be fulfilled. Only by betrayal, in a sense, could the promise be won.

This is a risky path, for it leaves the tried and true way of the collective. The great religions are containers providing protection from the fearful powers that can be unleased when the individual confronts himself. In my own view, the biblical tradition provides a constant safeguard against complete decompensation and loss of orientation. It's like a handrail on a slippery slope, and if you hold the rail with one hand you can go more safely into the depths of your own individuation process than you can without its support. If, on the other hand, you cling too tightly to the rail and stay too safe in your exploration, you won't come upon the greater treasures that lie in the dark beyond your vision. So I suggest that you proceed with the Bible in one hand and your own dream text in the other; hold fast to the ideals of justice and love while exploring the shadowy corners of envy and hatred; cling to the good even when enjoying the bad; sin boldly but remember God. And through this combination of tradition and individual experimentation with yourself, you will find yourself and the kingdom within and around you.

As the law was the master symbol for the first revelation of God, and the second was the Christ, the third is the concept of the self. As the Scripture for the first was the Hebrew Scriptures, particularly the Pentateuch, and for the second it was the New Testament, particularly the Gospels, for the third it is the individual's dreams. As the highest value left behind by the first revelation was justice and that of the second was love, the prime value of the third is wholeness. This is an evolutionary process, an individuation process for the collective, each stage of which is taken up in the next, included in it, and integrated by a larger circumference. Nothing of value is lost or left behind; all is enfolded and preserved in a greater unity.

PART II
The Gospel According to John

"Word"

If you're a writer, you know the problem of beginning. Every work has to start somewhere, and it quite often happens that one writes the beginning only later, or even last. This is because as an author you usually don't know what you're going to say until after you've put it on paper, and only then can you give it the proper send-off. As Pascal said, "The last thing one discovers in writing a book is what to put first." You want to say something at the outset that will set the stage and the tone, establish the main theme, and perhaps also connect the work to others in the same field or genre. You need to get the ball rolling. In Jungian analysis, we call the first dream brought to a session the "initial dream," and we pay careful attention to its implications. It signals "the beginning," and may forecast "the way" and even "the end."

Each of the four Gospels in the New Testament begins differently, and thus sets the stage for what follows accordingly. Matthew starts out by recounting in minute detail the ancestry of Jesus, tracing his line from Abraham, the ultimate father of the Hebrews. He establishes Jesus' credentials as a member of the people of Israel. (Still, it's somewhat odd, when you think about it, that this author would trace the ancestry of Jesus back to Abraham when he affirms only a short while later that Jesus' real progenitor is the Holy Spirit!) Mark begins by quoting the prophet Isaiah and setting the scene with the ministry of John the Baptist, who prepares the way for Jesus. Mark thus links Jesus to the prophetic tradition of the Old Testament and creates a sense of continuity with the spirituality of the previous books of the Bible. Luke, who wants to write a biographical account of the life and ministry of Jesus, begins with the story of John the Baptist's surprising conception, then moves to Jesus' even more miraculous conception, and then tells the most complete story of Jesus' human birth in a lowly manger in the town of Bethlehem. Like Matthew, Luke establishes the earthly lineage of Jesus as well as affirming his heavenly point of origin in the work of the Holy Spirit within the receptive womb and spirit of the young woman Mary. He emphasizes the humble human origins of the figure who will later be recognized as Lord.

The beginning of the Fourth Gospel is significantly different from those of the preceding three Gospels. Rather than establishing Jesus' earthly lineage in any fashion whatsoever, it leaps to the transcendent and references explicitly and exclusively his divine origin and nature. This author begins the story of Jesus' life at the beginning of time itself, before Jesus had a human face or human name. He is called "Word": "In the beginning was the Word: the Word was with God. He was with God in the beginning. Through him all things came to be. Not one thing had its being but through him. All that came to be had life in him and that life was the light of men, a light that shines in the dark, a light that darkness could not overpower."[72]

This opening of the story about Jesus' life on earth takes us all the way back to the very beginning of the biblical story

---

[72] John 1:1-5.

itself, to a point that antedates even Matthew's chronology, which extends back to the patriarch Abraham. The author of the fourth Gospel is emphasizing the divine identity of Jesus over his human identity, offering us a vision of Jesus' essence that identifies him with the Creator God of the Book of Genesis. The reference to Genesis 1:1 is unmistakable: "In the beginning God created the heavens and the earth."

John's opening lines restate the creation story and place the person who will be his chief subject, Jesus, right there at the beginning of all that is. His protagonist is a cosmic figure: "the Word" (Gr. *Logos*).

This opening to the narrative of Jesus' life does a number of things. Not only does it establish Jesus' credentials like the other three Gospels do in their own ways, but more important, it states at the very outset the essence of Jesus' identity and gives him an archetypal definition: he is superhuman. He is not only a teacher or a prophet like Isaiah or John the Baptist; he is God. But even more important, this opening of the story draws our attention back to the first sentence of the biblical narrative itself and defines Jesus as identical with the Creator God, Yahweh. He is Divine, but in a specific sense: he is not just any god or something vague like God-in-General, a principle of origination like the Big Bang. I underline this because it is important for establishing the precise meaning of this text. We are talking about the biblical God, Yahweh, as presented in the earlier accounts of Him as given in the Hebrew tradition and recorded in what has come to be called by Christians the Old Testament.

The Gospel of John is therefore intended to be a further revelation of the Divinity who has already been revealed throughout the biblical narrative. This is important to say because biblical scholars have debated the nature and sources of this Prologue, asking if John was incorporating a Gnostic myth to interpret the life and meaning of Jesus. Is the Word who was with God in the beginning to be identified with the Gnostic redeemer who comes from the realm of light into the darkness of this fallen world to reclaim our sparks of light, our souls, and lead them back to their point of origin in the other world? For our purposes here, it does not really matter whether the author of the fourth Gospel was influenced by Gnosticism or whether his Jesus is colored by the style and manner of the Essene sect who also spoke of an archetypal teacher. What does matter more is the context in which this particular text appears, because it is the cross references within the biblical narrative that supply us with the necessary associations to make our psychological interpretation. Without a context in which to interpret, the psychological interpreter can only speculate in a general way, and the interpretation loses its potential to convince.

If we were to find this Gospel all by itself on a shelf somewhere, outside of the biblical canon, we would be at a much greater loss than we are *with* the canonical context to understand what the author is trying to say with such terms as *Logos* ("Word"). With the context in mind, we can approach the meaning of the term, and therefore the meaning of the vision of this author, in a much more specific way.

I am following a rule of dream interpretation here, which says that each dream occurs within a psychological context. That context is made up of the lived experience of the individual dreamer, of his or her recent experiences, cultural background, and previous dreams. Each dream, each fantasy, in fact each piece of ideation or mental imagery, occurs within this particular context and must therefore be interpreted by taking the context into account. The context provides the associations needed to fill out the meaning of a dream image or idea.

We know little about the author of the fourth Gospel. Recent scholarship has established that this work is based on a preliterary tradition of oral reports and stories that is equally original as that behind the Synoptic Gospels, though perhaps somewhat separate and independent from that one. The actual identity of the writer of this text remains unknown. By tradition, the author is the disciple named John, who is identical with the one referred to in the text several times as "the beloved disciple." An argument has been put forward that the author is John Mark, not a disciple but an early follower of the apostles. Some have proposed Lazarus as the possible author. But it would not really help us much if we could positively identify the author because we would still know so little about his personal life and history, and as far as supplying a context for interpretation goes, you have to know quite a bit about the particular author in order to make use of those associations. So we are left with the contexts provided by the biblical narrative as a whole and by some historical knowledge of the times in which this work was composed. With that, plus our more general knowledge of symbolism which we can use to amplify the particular ideas and images of this text, we must make do.

All four Gospels, and all the books in the New Testament as well, are based on the premise that Jesus is special, more than human, and in fact the son of God. But no other text refers to him as "the Word" (*Logos*). Nor do the others place him in the beginning with, or as, the Creator as explicitly as does John. From a psychological interpretive viewpoint, this tells us that John is speaking of Jesus as an archetypal figure, that is, he is emphasizing the collective background more than his historical foreground. In psychology, the archetype is to ego-consciousness as the divine is to the human in mythology and theology: a basic structural element and dynamic, an essence that is there at the beginning, pre-conscious, and as far as we can know, "eternal." Our knowledge is limited to the finite, so we cannot say for sure that archetypes are eternal, but we do say that they establish the essential nature of what it is to have a human mind and psyche. They are the basic building blocks of the human psyche, and Jung also speculated that they may correspond to the basic structures of reality, which lie beyond the human mind and its knowing.

In taking a psychological approach, we must limit ourselves to the psychological horizon, and so it is within this framework that we say that the fourth Gospel opens by stating that the subject is an archetypal image. By this, the author is pointing beyond time and history and is speaking of ultimate powers and final structures. The author is speaking of the meaning of the Jesus event.

As a term, *logos* does not say "archetype," but the way John uses it fixes it in that sense. The term is an anomaly in the biblical text as a whole. No-one else uses it. It is a Greek word that means "word" or "order," and it has a traditional usage in Greek philosophy. But John is not simply borrowing from Greek philosophy to amplify the meaning of Jesus, although he may wish to create an echo for his Greek audience. For the Greeks, *logos* meant rational orderliness, and there is no indication that John is using it in this sense. Nor does the term have roots in the Old Testament. So John is using a fresh word as far as the biblical context is concerned, and this, of course, highlights his approach. We automatically pay attention to something new and out of place in a familiar context. John is saying that there is a new archetypal image that has come into consciousness, and he wants to tell us about it. But it is not simply new, since it is an extension of the previous archetypal image of Yahweh that has been making its way into consciousness since the beginning of the biblical narrative. John is announcing a new vision of something that was there all along but is only now coming into awareness. It is new and not new.

This is the nature of revelation. Something that has been there all along but has been hidden or implicit has now come into focus and is made explicit. What was once invisible can now be seen. Translated into psychological language, John is saying that an archetypal image, which was there all along but lay hidden in the unconscious, has now come into awareness, and that this is an aspect of the same archetypal content that was known before as the symbol of a transcendent identity (Yahweh), only now, through the events recorded in this Gospel, it can be known. It has become more conscious. It is a new revelation.

The notion that an invisible and heretofore unknown spiritual figure becomes incarnated and lives among humans on a physical and observable plane is a statement that signifies what is psychologically understood to be an entry into consciousness. Genesis begins with the story of emergent consciousness. The archetypal power named Yahweh creates consciousness by instituting distinctions: dividing light from darkness, water from dry land, and earth below from firmament above. God creates specifically human conscious-ness by forming man and woman in his own image. In this fashion, He reveals Himself. Humans are "in His own image." Creation stories are stories of coming to consciousness, of waking up, of developing awareness and cognitive functions. This brings with it the beginnings of a sense of identity within, and a sense of stable definitions of the various objects in the surrounding world.

Now, at the beginning of the fourth Gospel, we find a second biblical creation story, a second coming to consciousness of an archetypal image, which in some way repeats the first and original one but adds a further dimension. This is not a matter of recreating the original consciousness that dawned at the beginning of time and human awareness, or of tribal identity, but rather of creating more precise consciousness of the Creative Being Himself. The Creator is coming into better focus and further into human consciousness. The origin or archetype of this particular consciousness, which has acted in the development of the biblical narrative, is itself now coming into consciousness. This means that human consciousness is being expanded and is now able to take further into account the source of its being. The ego is becoming aware of the self, to use Jungian language. This ego-consciousness can now know what had not been known before: precisely, the image and essence of its creator and of its point of origin. This is a huge leap in self-consciousness and the potential for a more inclusive identity.

It is also a matter of the archetype itself becoming conscious of itself in a new way. In other words, God becomes more conscious of His nature. The distance between archetype and ego-consciousness has been closed, and both sides of this equation are affected by this development. The author of the fourth Gospel is much too modest, of course, to presume such an implication of what he is saying. His emphasis lies and remains on the added knowledge we have of Him:

"The Word was made flesh,
he lived among us,[73]
and we saw his glory,
the glory that is his as the only Son of the Father,
full of grace and truth."[74]

This is, I believe, the core of John's message. In the life
and death and teaching of Jesus, he saw the glory of God; he
saw the same numinous presence that confronted Moses at
the burning bush and named himself "I am." He saw the
glory of the God who spoke to the prophets, about whom
King David sang his Psalms, who was there at the beginning
creating heaven and earth. The "Word" is to be identified
with "God," and this revelation will further define the
meaning of the word "God" for humankind.

In the hands of this author, "the Word" is a symbol that
refers to an experience of numinous vision in which God
was revealed concretely in the person of Jesus. Word, Jesus,
and Yahweh are equivalent terms, so that what you say of one
you can and must say of the others, and what you see in one
you can attribute without remainder to the others. There is
nothing about Jesus that is not of a piece with the essence of
Yahweh, for he is Yahweh. He can therefore reveal the essence
and meaning of Yahweh for humankind concretely and
tangibly.

And yet the text also says that he is the Son of the
Father, as though Yahweh still stands behind him, reserved
and beyond. John is going to walk in this paradox throughout
his Gospel: Jesus is one with the Father, comes from the

---

[73] Lit. "pitched his tent among us," *The Jerusalem Bible*, John 1:14, ftn. n.
[74] John 1:14.

Father, speaks for the Father, does nothing that is not of the Father, and is utterly identical in every way with the Father, yet the Father remains elsewhere, impervious and eternal. Jesus as "the Word" is a symbol of the Father, and yet, the archetype lies somewhere beyond the human image – the incarnate form.

I don't think we should take this to mean that there is any difference between the symbol and the underlying reality as far as meaning or intention is concerned, but perhaps we can assume that something remains to be revealed that is not yet revealed in this image. This will come later in the "third person" of the Trinity, but for the moment, Jesus is a full and complete revelation of Yahweh. Yahweh is eternal in a way that flesh and blood are not: the archetype can be revealed in a particular image but is not confined to that image. The archetype can appear in other images, too: in other persons or in other times and places. No one owns the archetype; it owns itself. The archetype exists beyond individual appropriations or revelations or images.

My way of thinking about the meaning of the term "*Logos*," or "Word," is as "pattern of spiritual meaning." My translation runs: "In the beginning was the spiritual pattern and the pattern was of God and the pattern was God." This pattern is revealed and given content in the biblical narrative about Yahweh and in the figure of Jesus. In the life, teachings, and gestures of Jesus, we can see the pattern of transcendent meaning, John tells us, which is the same pattern as was there in the beginning when Yahweh created the first glimmerings of consciousness and biblical identity. It is also the same pattern of meaning and divine will as was revealed to the fathers Abraham, Isaac, and Jacob; the same that is revealed in the story of the Passover, the tablets given to Moses, and in the wilderness. It is the same as revealed in the Law. In Jesus we can see more of this same pattern clearly, specifically, and concretely. This is an aspect that was not revealed so clearly before, but make no mistake, what we see in Jesus is the same fundamental pattern that has set the biblical identity and defined its meaning from the beginning of the history of the biblical people.

If Jesus' divine identity is rather hidden and only gradually and carefully revealed in the Gospel of Mark, in John's Gospel it is unveiled from the outset. From the start to the finish of this Gospel, the message is proclaimed that Jesus and the Father are one and that Jesus is the revelation of the Father without parallel. Jesus reveals Yahweh by his teaching, his gestures, and his generously creative life. There is abundance and life wherever he goes. The water of life flows from his very pores. The bulk of the Gospel is made up of stories about Jesus that fill in the details of the divine pattern and give it emotional vividness. We are learning about the personality of God. For those who have only the text and not the experience of meeting Jesus in the flesh, these words of the Gospel are the portrait of the divine incarnation. They detail and spell out the pattern we are supposed to comprehend. If in the Hebrew Scriptures, Yahweh reveals himself most explicitly in the Law and the Torah and the words of the prophets, in the New Testament, He is revealed by Jesus who incarnates Him.

What is it about Jesus that is so revelatory? What does he reveal? Many of the stories about him are meant to show his superhuman power: he can perform miracles like turning water into wine and healing the sick, even raising the dead. But these are merely signs that are intended to prove his credentials, as it were, as the son of God. Chapters 2-12 of the Gospel are devoted to these signs. The distinguished Roman Catholic biblical scholar, Raymond Brown, calls this part of the Gospel the "Book of Signs." These signs reveal Jesus' power over nature, which is impressive, but they do not in themselves tell us anything we would not have known about God before. Yahweh performed similar miracles in Egypt and the wilderness. The signs serve to solidify and prove the identity of Jesus and Yahweh, but they do not reveal anything new.

On the other hand, chapters 11-20 of the fourth Gospel, which Brown calls the "Book of Glory," are made up of quite different content. Here we find Jesus at the Last Supper giving his discourses and teachings and then going out to be tried, judged, and crucified. This is followed by his resurrection and the so-called resurrection appearances. Finally there is a brief epilogue made up of several more post-resurrection appearances. Somewhere in this material is the revelation, the opening up to consciousness of a deep, still unconscious mystery about the nature of the archetypal pattern, the God personality, that is named the Word and is Yahweh.

There are a number of key episodes in this material where, I believe, this deep revelation takes place. The first is in the foot-washing scene in chapter 13; the second is in his teaching about the "true vine" and in Jesus' conversion of the master-disciple relationship to one of friendship (chapter 15), and the third is the Passion itself. The three of these, taken together, lead us to what I believe to be the central, and surprising, features of the archetypal pattern being revealed by Jesus.

I look for a "surprise" on the assumption that if one already knew something consciously one would not need a revelation. In dream interpretation, we apply the same rule:

if you already know something consciously, you don't need to dream about it. If the message of the dream seems to be something you know already, then you haven't understood the dream yet. Dreams, like revelations, come from an area of the mind outside of conscious awareness, from the unconscious, and they add something to the contents of consciousness.

In the materials I mentioned, Jesus shows himself to be the servant of his followers (in the act of foot-washing), teaches them that he is their friend and not their master who like a good friend is willing to lay down his life for his friends, and then finally submits without resistance to the humiliating death by crucifixion in accordance with the pattern of the suffering servant as described by the Old Testament prophets. This pattern of service, friendship, and accepted suffering is what Jesus most clearly and dramatically reveals.

The basic statement of the Gospel is that God is "loving service." This belongs centrally to the divine pattern that underlies biblical consciousness and consequent biblical identity. At work in the psychic background here in John's Gospel is a tremendous shift in emergent consciousness, however, and in this respect, we have to think of the biblical narrative as the story of an unfolding individuation process while the archetypal image comes into consciousness over the centuries. It is not a static image, but rather, a gradual display of various features. As the features emerge, ego-consciousness and identity change and evolve. The consciousness that had formed in the beginning of the life of the ancient Hebrews through being led out of Egypt and given the Law, then through establishing a kingdom in the promised land and building a temple, and finally through refining a religion for everyday life that was separate and distinct from all the other religions in the area was now undergoing a further transformation. In the earlier perspective, Yahweh had been established as a Law Giver, a God of justice, and a king figure. He was the Lord of Lords. In Jesus, one sees a significantly different image. When Jesus is called King of the Jews, it is with disrespectful irony. What kind of a king is this who suffers passively and dies with thieves on a cross? This is a divine personality who proclaims love and brotherhood and service, indeed one who shows these qualities in the way he lives, rather than merely demonstrating power and control and regal superiority.

This is the surprise of the revelation and the scandal. Because it is so different from what one would expect of an epiphany of Yahweh – the sky god, the fierce warrior God who takes no prisoners, the jealous God – it was necessary for John to emphasize the identity between Jesus, the Word, and Yahweh. This is why he is so insistent throughout his Gospel on the identity of Jesus and the Father.

It was indeed anything but self-evident to the Pharisees and priests that Jesus resembled Yahweh, let alone defined Him, or that the pattern he revealed was the same divine One they worshiped at the temple in Jerusalem. Therefore, it had to be strongly emphasized and insisted upon by the New Testament writers, especially by John. In truth, this was a new vision of the biblical God, and for all the claims made for continuity and sameness, the divine pattern was revealing something new: a set of features that had been concealed and had not been strongly emphasized before. The difference was great enough to inspire a new direction in the Hebrew religion – one not completely cut off from the prior one, but different enough to warrant a whole new set of doctrines and understandings.

The Christians were about creating a new consciousness based primarily on the pattern as revealed by Jesus. Imitatio

Christi: This pattern of humility and service, rather than kingship and dominance, would be their model as they set out to tell the world about their revelation of God.

Reading backward from the revelation of God in Christ, the ancient Scriptures showed implicit traces of this pattern in the earlier epiphanies, especially as recorded in the Psalms and in the Prophets. As a "type," Christ would be found in subtle manifestation throughout the biblical narrative. But now it was plain: one could see clearly. The Gospels spell out the pattern as revealed in the incarnation of God in Jesus.

Nietzsche disdained the Christian God image in favor of the more noble and heroic Greek gods. He saw only sickness in this dying and passive image of God. What would we say, psychologically speaking, about a type of consciousness and identity molded by this archetype of suffering and service? Were Nietzsche a modern psychiatrist, he might speak of masochism or some such psychopathology. And surely there are instances of individuals who are drawn to this Christian pattern out of such distorting impulses. But at its best and healthiest, the expression of this archetypal constellation in life presents us with a person who is able to put others ahead of his or her own needs when necessary, who is able to be generous and to share, who has mastered narcissism and envy for the sake of relationship, and who is directed by a purpose that Erik Erikson named generativity and Jung spoke of as the constellation of the transcendent function.

The transcendent function, according to Jung's theoretical formulation, is a psychic structure that allows for a certain amount of detachment from the ego and from egoistic claims and identifications. It allows even for some detachment from one's pet ideas and compulsions, one's so-called rational attitudes. It creates an open space in consciousness for receiving the words and viewpoints of other voices (inner and outer) and, if need be, for giving up one's own preferences for the larger good of a relationship or commitment.

In developmental terms, this stage of individuation lies beyond the earlier stage of heroic ego development, which is, however, seen as a necessary precursor. Jesus, dramatically demonstrating the possibility for a constellation of the transcendent function within the human psyche, reveals a stage of development beyond that of legalism, heroism, and even mature kingship and rulership. Nietzsche was actually advocating for a regression in individuation by proposing the Greek ideal of active striving for perfection, which is an ego ideal.

Unfortunately, the Christian stage of individuation may be so advanced, developmentally speaking, that few individuals can genuinely attain it in their lives. For it is not a matter of effort and ego-struggle for perfection that one attains to the Christ pattern. To reach it, one would have to replicate in some inner and psychological way the developmental process outlined in the biblical narrative, from creation of ego consciousness through the separation stage, the warrior stage, the kingship stage, to the first inklings of the transcendent function in the prophetic stage, and finally its fully embodied conscious realization in the Christ stage. But this is, I believe, the revelation that John witnessed in his beloved friend, Jesus, to which he bears such eloquent and persuasive witness in his Gospel.

The "Word" of the fourth Gospel symbolizes the biblical God image in a new stage of its emergence in the four-square, time and space world of ego-consciousness. While this is a glorious spectacle, it also creates the potential for a sharp division between good and evil in the psyche, as we shall see in the next lecture.

"Light"

Kierkegaard asked a pointed existential question: Would you have been a follower of Jesus if you had lived in his time? We might equally wonder: If we had lived in the days of Socrates, would we have listened to his claims or would we have heeded the warning of those who said he was corrupting the youth of Athens? History is replete with examples of conflict between established groups and those who challenge their position, authority and legitimacy. Whose side do you typically take? It's a personal decision, and Jesus was famous for calling people to make a choice. So was Moses. And so was Yahweh. This is what the Bible is all about.

In the fourth Gospel, the main issue that divides those who follow Jesus from those who do not is the matter of trust in his claims that he comes from the Father, that he is one with the Father, and that he is "the Way, the Truth, and the Life." Either you accept this claim, or you don't. There is no middle ground. "Trust me," Jesus says. "Believe in me and you will be saved; deny me and reject my claims, and you are lost." Discipleship for John amounts to just one thing: trust in Jesus. This demands the famous Kierkegaardian "leap of faith."

The other three Gospels also divide those who follow Jesus from those who don't, but not quite as sharply and not exactly along the same axis. For Matthew, the emphasis falls on obedience to "the new law" announced by Jesus. The Kingdom of God, which Jesus describes in poetic detail and brings with him into this time-and-space world, introduces a new set of rules. Jesus spells this new law out in his Sermon on the Mount and other teachings, and discipleship requires following these rules. If you want to be a disciple of Jesus, learn the beatitudes and let them be your guide. Mathew continues the tradition of the good Jew who heeds the Commandments given to Moses and the laws derived from them. Similarly, in Mark and Luke, discipleship requires taking up your cross and following him, selling what you have and giving to the poor, risking your life so that you may find it, etc. In none of the synoptic Gospels is the emphasis so squarely placed on trust in Jesus' claims to divine identity as it is in John's Gospel.

John's is the most inward of the four Gospels. The author plays down the importance of outward behavior in favor of a state of mind anchored in faith and trust. In his so-called Discourses, Jesus invites his twelve disciples to merge with him, to become one with him as he is one with the father, as branches are one with the vine that provides them with access to nourishment.[75] There is less emphasis on obedience to rules and laws here and more on trust and intimate relationship. The relationship between Jesus and his disciples in the fourth Gospel is, among the four accounts, portrayed as the most intimate.

The remarkable intimacy between Jesus and his disciples in the fourth Gospel parallels Jesus' intimacy with the Father, inviting the disciples into a state of psychological merger and union. This is dramatized in the lengthy account

---

[75] John 15:1-11.

of the Last Supper. Not only through the words of Jesus, but also in the description of the physicality of his gestures and body language, the author conveys an atmosphere of erotic intimacy that is striking, especially considering that the twelve disciples are robust and untutored working men. In developmental terms, these scenes are "pre-Oedipal," i.e., erotic not in the genital sense but in the earlier maternal sense. Jesus is shown as an embracing, nurturing figure, inviting his twelve children to become intimate with him one last time before he takes his leave. Like a good mother, he prepares them for the coming separation, and lovingly, he lingers on this moment for a long time. He does not hurry off the way men typically tend to do. He comforts them, he bathes them, he feeds them, and he tells them he is preparing a place for them where they will be able to rejoin him later.

> "My little children,
> I shall not be with you much longer.
> You will look for me,
> and, as I told the Jews,
> where I am going,
> you cannot come.
> I give you a new commandment:
> love one another;
> just as I have loved you,
> you also must love one another.
> By this love you have for one another,
> Everyone will know that you are my disciples."[76]

---

[76] John 13:33-35.

This is the "love commandment," and it is pronounced within the nurturing aura of maternal reassurance. The words in this passage are typical of the last discourses, which one must hear spoken by Jesus in an intimate voice, in the night, to his closest disciples, now called his friends. This is a time of final bonding among them, and in these moments together he knits them firmly to himself so that when he leaves they will not forget and go after others looking for a substitute. They will be able to wait for him. Through these acts and words of intimate love, Jesus imprints the disciples indelibly with his image, the way a mother would her child or a lover his beloved. It is no accident that bathing and feeding are a part, in fact are the central gestures, of this scene, which extends remarkably over five chapters (13-17) of the fourth Gospel and is unparalleled in the synoptic Gospels.

Foot washing, as it is commonly recognized by commentators and interpreters, is a sign of humility and servanthood, and this gesture is used by the author to illustrate the essence of Jesus' archetypal identity as servant. But it is also dramatically intimate. There are not many recorded instances of physical contact between Jesus and his followers. This is one. Here he touches the feet of each one of his disciples, washing them and wiping them. There were earlier instances of Jesus having his feet washed; only a chapter earlier Mary had anointed his feet with expensive nard, for which she was duly criticized by Judas Iscariot and defended by Jesus with the famous and often misused line, "The poor you have with you always." Now we see Jesus tenderly bathing his disciples' feet. What a powerful bonding image, to see the Master carefully handling those rather gross, earthy appendages of the human body. And when Peter, who out of false humility which is actually masked pride, protests with, "You shall never wash my feet," Jesus demands submission to this bonding gesture: "If I do not wash you, you can have nothing in common with me."[77] Unless he handles your feet, you are not bonded to him.

It is amazing that a text which begins so abstractly with the sentence, "In the beginning was the Word," should then be able to make its way to a scene so diametrically opposite as this one is, so concrete, physical, specific, and tenderly loving. The fourth Gospel holds the tension of the opposites Logos and Eros. They are united in the figure of the Gospel's protagonist. Both belong to his essential identity and nature. Logos is the form, Eros the content of this archetypal figure.

The Last Supper scene has been depicted by artists countless times, most famously by Leonardo da Vinci. Scholars have tried to reconstruct the seating arrangement at this paschal meal. F. Prat suggested the arrangement of the Roman triclinium, with three couches in a squared-off horseshoe pattern and arranged around a central table.[78] Five disciples would be sitting on the two side couches, and two with Jesus at the head couch, the "*lectus medius.*" The text says that "the disciple Jesus loved,"[79] often thought to be John, the author of this Gospel, was reclining next to Jesus, probably on his right. The scene is cast as high psychological drama. In the midst of the love feast, the devil makes an appearance. After washing the disciples' feet, Jesus becomes "troubled in spirit" and says, "I tell you most solemnly, one

---

[77] John 13:6-8.
[78] Cited by Raymond Brown, *The Gospel According to John: The Anchor Bible* (New York, London: Doubleday, 1970), 574.
[79] John 13:23.

of you will betray me."[80] Suddenly the mood shifts, from the intimacy of foot washing and the exhortations to humility and discipleship, to fear. Jesus is troubled, his emotions stirred up by his knowledge of the coming event of betrayal. Betrayal is most deeply disturbing when the bonds of trust have seemingly been formed. The feet of all twelve have been handled by Jesus, each of them therefore presumably bonded to him in tender intimacy and care. Then, suddenly, the subject of betrayal arises. Psychologically and dramatically, the timing is arresting.

This notion that he is about to be betrayed is not a paranoid thought. Jesus knows it's coming. The disciple whom Jesus loved, who is reclining next to him, is asked by Peter, who must be at some distance and does not feel close enough himself to ask, to find out from Jesus who this betrayer is. So, "leaning back on Jesus breast (note the physicality and the exactness of the location touched) he says, 'Who is it lord?'" And Jesus replies, I suppose in a close whisper so the betrayer will not overhear him, "It is the one to whom I give the piece of bread that I shall dip in the dish." Then Jesus dips the bread in the oil and gives it to Judas, son of Simon Iscariot, who must also be sitting nearby (Raymond Brown thinks he may be reclining to Jesus' left, a place of honor that would be his by virtue of his being the treasurer of the group.) Here again, we witness these physical gestures – John leaning against Jesus' breast, Jesus hand-feeding the disciples – in the midst of a mood of nurturing and dark betrayal. At that very instant, as though the scene were suddenly lit up by a flash of lightening, and "after Judas had taken the bread, Satan entered him," Jesus says, "What you

---

[80] John 13:21.

are going to do, do quickly."[81] Judas leaves stealthily, night falls, and Jesus says to the remaining eleven:

"Now has the Son of Man been glorified,
and in him God has been glorified.
If God has been glorified in him,
God will in turn glorify him in himself,
And will glorify him very soon."[82]

At this moment of physical darkness and psychological betrayal, the light shines most brightly.

"Glory" is the manifestation of God's presence – the light spoken of throughout the Gospel and prefigured in the Hebrew Scriptures. As John says in the prologue: "The Word was made flesh, he lived among us, and we saw his glory, the glory that is his as the only Son of the Father, full of grace and truth."[83] Over against this glory and light there is the darkness. There are those who accept the light and there are those who reject it and live in darkness. There is the one who is the light and brings the light, the Word, Jesus; and there is the darkness which resists the light and tries to overpower it but fails. "The Word was the true light that enlightens all men; and he was coming into the world. He was now in the world that had its being through him, and the world did not know him. He came to his own domain and his own people did not accept him. But to all who did accept him he gave the power to become children of God, to all who believe in

---

[81] John 13:27.
[82] John 13:31-32.
[83] John 1:14.

the name of him who was born not out of human stock or urge of the flesh or will of man but of God himself."[84]

Commentators speak of the dualism in the fourth Gospel and suggest Zoroastrian and other possible influences. In many of the world's religions and mythologies there is a battle between dark and light forces and their various agents. In modern times, in movies like "Star Wars," we find this same structure of imagery and thinking. It is an inevitable by-product of emerging consciousness.

In the biblical narrative, the first discrimination of consciousness is between light and dark: God said, "Let there be light and there was light. God saw that light was good, and God divided light from darkness. God called light 'day,' and darkness he called 'night.' Evening came and morning came: the first day."[85] The kind of consciousness created at the outset of the biblical narrative is clear, crisp, and consequently, also divisive. If you draw a sharp line, you create two sides. When light is separated from dark, they are two distinct states. When you choose one people from among all the others of the earth, you have created the chosen as well as the not-chosen. When a set of laws is promulgated, you have created the possibility of crime. God began this process of discrimination between right and wrong in Paradise when He told Adam and Eve that they could eat of any tree but two were out of bounds and forbidden. By forbidding these, He created the division between obedience and disobedience.

Biblical consciousness is sharply delineated, and this mind became schooled in refined discriminations. It is the

---

[84] John 1:9-13.

[85] Genesis 1:3-5.

function of the Judges first, and later of the prophets, to hold
the plumb line taut and to measure the extent and degree of
moral and religious infraction. The consolidation of this type
of a strong moral and ethical consciousness is sufficient
background for the drama between light and darkness in the
fourth Gospel without having to resort to myths and
religions further afield. The fourth Gospel, moreover, does
not show evidence of a full blown mythical battle between
the forces of light and the forces of darkness. The light is in
firm control, and the darkness is, if anything, used to add
contrast to the light. So it is that when Satan entered Judas,
he is actually following the destiny assigned to him by God
and glorifying Jesus rather than seriously challenging him.
There is no real contest, and Satan is, if anything, a minion.

Yet, in John's Gospel there is an extremely sharp line
of demarcation between light and dark, belief and unbelief,
and true and false claims. The author of the Gospel sees in
Jesus a new archetype emerging into consciousness, and this
challenges the old structures of consciousness. It is a battle
between the new consciousness and the old, between faith
in this new figure who has come into the world just recently
and claims to be God and to speak directly for God, and
those who remain loyal to the ancient tradition of Scripture,
belief, interpretation, and practice. This is the struggle
between light and darkness: the light is the new consciousness, and the dark is the ignorance of it, the unconsciousness,
or the unwillingness to receive it as valid. Those who walk
in darkness and choose to stay in darkness do so because they
cannot see, do not understand, are ignorant, asleep, or blind.
Actually, they are entrenched in their past commitments,
identifications, and beliefs. They are the establishment.

The major division in the Gospel is between Jesus and his few followers on the one hand and "the Jew" on the other. We have to put "Jews" in quotation marks because all of the characters in the story are Jews in the genetic sense. Jesus is as much a Jew as Annas and Caiaphas who condemn him to death, and the disciples are Jews as well. But they do not fall into the category of "the Jews" as John defines them. "The Jews" are the ones who do not believe that Jesus is the Son of God or God Himself. In a remarkable dialogue with "the Jews," which occupies the greater part of chapter 8 of the Gospel, Jesus tells them about his identity and then goes on to define this identity by contrast. "The Jews" claim to be Abraham's children, that is, among the chosen of God, and Jesus argues with them on this point:

> "If you were Abraham's children, you would do as Abraham did.
> As it is, you want to kill me when I tell you the truth as I have learnt it from God; that is not what Abraham did.
> What you are doing is what your father does."

> They reply; "We were not born of prostitution... we have one father: God."

> To which Jesus answers:
> "If God were your father, you would love me,
> since I have come here from God; yes, I have come from him;
> not that I came because I chose,
> no, I was sent, and by him.
> Do you know why you cannot take in what I say?
> It is because you are unable to understand my language.

The devil is your father, and you prefer to do what your father wants.
He was a murderer from the start; he was never grounded in the truth; there is no truth in him at all: when he lies he is drawing on his own store, because he is a liar, and the father of lies.
But as for me, I speak the truth and for that very reason, you do not believe me."[86]

The emotional tone of the argument is clearly escalating. As things become more emotional, "the Jews" finally call Jesus possessed, insane. Jesus continues calling them liars and the children of the Father of all lies, while claiming that his father is the true God of the biblical tradition, the God of Abraham. Finally, Jesus resorts to telling them about his pre-existent condition in heaven:

"Your father Abraham rejoiced
to think that he would see my Day;
he saw it and was glad."
The Jews then said, 'You are not fifty yet, and you have seen Abraham!' Jesus replied:
"I tell you most solemnly,
before Abraham ever was,
I Am."

With that, Jesus defines himself as God, "I Am," as the God who revealed Himself to Moses at the burning bush.
Now clearly, "the Jews," who stand for the given tradition of belief and practice among the population of the times had grounds for thinking they were dealing with a

[86] John 8:39-45.

madman. Wouldn't you, if someone argued emotionally that he had lived before his earthly birth in heaven with the patriarchs, and even before them as God? We lock these people up today and treat them with anti-psychotic drugs. So I return to Kierkegaard's question: Would you be a follower of Jesus if you had lived then, or if one such as Jesus appeared today? Clearly, the gospel writer thought it was the enlightened thing to do to believe Jesus' claims. He was one whose eyes were open, he could see the glory of Christ, while others saw only a lunatic. We would say today that he had an archetypal transference to Jesus, that he was projecting the self on him and therefore was prepared to believe these extreme claims. There were few enough who did, finally only twelve, and one of those was a betrayer.

The author of the fourth Gospel presents another figure, who is a sort of balancing figure, one who does not become polarized in this conflict between old and new consciousness, and one who, while he remains loyal to tradition, listens and empathizes with the emergent new force. I am referring to that remarkable figure who appears only in the fourth Gospel, Nicodemus. I take this figure to be an expression of the need on the part of the biblical psyche to contain the violent tension of the opposites and to keep itself intact in the midst of what we see in the fourth Gospel as an intensely polarized situation: light vs. darkness, Jesus vs. "the Jews," love vs. hatred, and the new vs. the old. The hostility is all the more intense for the emphasis on love, the dark all the darker because the light is brighter. While John's is the Gospel of Love, it is also the story of equally intense emotional antagonism and resistance. This is a story of crisis in which the exponent of new consciousness and a transformed attitude confronts the entrenched exponents of a solidified tradition. This attempt to introduce a transformative change first produces a violent crisis, as the intensity of opposition equals the intensity of the force for change. Every light-bringer runs into this, and murderous rage and execution is not a surprising conclusion to the story. A parallel in Greek mythology is found in the story of Prometheus, the Titan who stole fire ("light") from the gods and shared it with humans and for that was nailed to the Caucasus mountains and violently attacked every night by the eagle of Zeus, who was in this case the entrenched power.

Nicodemus appears as a gentle, intelligent, humane, curious figure. In his first appearance in the Gospel, he comes to Jesus at night and inquires about his teachings. He recognizes that Jesus is sent from God because of his demonstrated powers. In the dialogue between Nicodemus and Jesus, whom he addresses as "Rabbi," we have some of the most memorable sayings of Jesus in the entire Gospel. Jesus teaches Nicodemus about the spiritual transformation he is inaugurating:

> "I tell you most solemnly,
> unless a man is born from above,
> he cannot see the kingdom of God...
> unless a man is born through water and the Spirit,
> he cannot enter the kingdom of God:
> what is born of the flesh is flesh;
> what is born of the Spirit is spirit.
> Do not be surprised when I say:
> You must be born from above."[87]

Jesus speaks to Nicodemus about eternal life, about God's love, and about his mission on earth:

---

[87] John 3:3-7.

"Yes, God loved the world so much
that he gave his only Son,
so that everyone who believes in him may not be lost
but may have eternal life."[88]

Every "born again" Christian knows these verses by heart (in the King James translation, most likely). Among the most memorable lines in the entire Bible, these are addressed to the one solitary Pharisee who would listen to Jesus. The writer does not tell us what Nicodemus' reaction was to these words, but when he makes his next appearance in the Gospel it is evident that he did not leave his identity as a Pharisee and join the disciples. But, from that position, he plays a noteworthy role.

In his second appearance, he reveals his balanced and judicious attitude. When the police are sent to bring Jesus before the high priests, they come back without him and are questioned:

"'Why haven't you brought him?' The police replied, 'There has never been anybody who has spoken like him.' 'So' the Pharisees answered 'you have been led astray as well? Have any of the authorities believed in him? Any of the Pharisees? This rabble knows nothing about the Law – they are damned.' One of them, Nicodemus – the same man who had come to Jesus earlier – said to them, 'But surely the Law does not allow us to pass judgement on a man without giving him a hearing and discovering what he is about?' To this they answered, 'Are you a Galilean too? Go into the matter, and see for yourself: prophets do not come out of Galilee.'"[89]

---

[88] John 3:16.
[89] John 7:45-52.

The argument of the Pharisees here is dogmatic: prophets do not come out of Galilee, period, by definition. The argument of Nicodemus, who has been exposed to the persuasive power of Jesus' message, perhaps reflects that some of this has had its effect. At least he did not come away from the encounter thinking Jesus was a madman or a criminal. Nicodemus would represent the liberal element within the ruling party, and had he had a stronger voice in the party the outcome of the conflict between Jesus and "the Jews" might have been entirely different. Nicodemus would have sought accommodation, treating Jesus as a prophet sent from God in the tradition of Isaiah and Jeremiah. But would Jesus have accepted this definition of himself and his ministry? Would he have been satisfied to be seen as just another of a whole string of prophets in this long tradition? Nothing in the Gospels gives us grounds for thinking so. Jesus' challenge was too radical, his claims of a different order. Nicodemus' middle-of-the-road moderation and openness to possible new elements appearing in consciousness, in the collective culture of the day, is doomed to failure in a starkly divided situation like the one depicted in the Gospels. There is no middle ground to stand on. During a time of profound transition, the middle is swept away. Perhaps it can reappear later in history, among the liberal and humane theologians of both Judaism and Christianity some centuries later. But in the time of division and crisis, when a new archetype of consciousness is confronting the en-trenched ways and habits of a settled consciousness, a tradition, a fixed culture, compromise and accommodation are impossible. It is a power struggle to the death, and there must be a winner and a loser. Only later, when the dust of conflict had settled, the new Christian tradition would be able to propose a degree of reconciliation by joining its New

Testament to the ancient Hebrew Scriptures in a single canon. In this formal act there was an acknowledgment of continuity, but still it was a harmonization in which the New continued to outweigh the Old in value.

Nicodemus makes a brief third appearance in the Johannine version of the burial of Jesus. Joseph of Arimathaea, a secret follower of Jesus, asks Pilate for permission to remove and bury the body. Pilate consents, and Joseph takes the body away. "Nicodemus came as well – the same one who had first come to Jesus at night-time – and he brought a mixture of myrrh and aloes, weighing about a hundred pounds."[90] Perhaps Nicodemus was convinced by Jesus after all and, like Joseph of Arimathaea, thought of himself as a secret disciple. Perhaps you and I, had we lived at the time and been put in a position of having to decide about Jesus and his claims, would have reacted like Nicodemus: hesitant, inquiring, hoping for accommodation, secretly convinced by the movement of the spirit within. But certainly, had we listened to the claims of Jesus and the arguments of the Pharisees, we would have been torn and divided. The New Testament is a book of and about crisis, the kind of crisis that is a part of every major shift in consciousness and psychological development, whether individual and personal or cultural and collective. Jesus is the light, the bringer of new consciousness, the change-agent, who also creates division and throws the psyche into the liminal state of transition. It is in this state of liminality that "the Way" must be found.

---

[90] John 19:39.

"Way"

"The way is ineffable," Jung once wrote. "One cannot, one must not, betray it. It is like the way of Zen – like a sharp knife, and also twisting like a serpent. One needs faith, courage, and no end to honesty and patience."[91] John's Gospel also speaks of "the way" and offers directions for finding it. "I am the way..." Jesus says in reply to Thomas' query, "Lord, we do not know where you are going, so how can we know the way?"[92] It seems evident that one major purpose in John's Gospel is to communicate this message, that a new light has dawned, a new consciousness and identity has offered itself, a new way to the Divine has been found. This is the revelation. Whatever else the meaning of the life and death of Jesus might have been, it was, for the author of the fourth Gospel, the presentation of the way.

In liminality, one needs to find a sense of the way. The Gospels were written in retrospect, after some years of reflection and mulling it all over had passed. They are therefore a mixture of reportage and interpretation, and what they communicate to us is a symbol. A symbol is a fact plus its meaning, communicated in such a way that the reality

---

[91] C.G. Jung, *C.G. Jung Speaking*, William McGuire and R.F.C. Hull (eds.) (Princeton, NJ: Princeton University Press, 1977), 361.
[92] John 14:5. *The Jerusalem Bible.*

to which it intends to direct us also becomes accessible. This is a symbol that will work for others. Uncommunicated, it could be a private symbol, lost as far as the generality is concerned. The writers of the Gospels were trying to pass along the symbol to others, eventually to us.

All New Testament authors agree upon the point that it was important, indeed necessary, for Jesus both to live and to die in the way he did. There is nothing accidental about either his life, his ministry or his manner and time of death. All of it belongs to a divine plan. And it is this divine plan that the authors wish to communicate and wish to have the readers and hearers of their narratives respond to with faith and trust. As John has Jesus asking his listeners to believe that he comes from the Father and indeed is one with God, so John would want his readers to do the same.

In John's view, Jesus was a man who originated in the divine realms, came to earth for the purpose of showing the light, the truth, and the way, and after his death returned to the home he had come from. Everything that he said and did, and everything that happened to him while he was on earth in the flesh, was part of a plan and under the direction and control of the heavenly Father. While his troubles and trials on earth were severe ones from a human point of view, they were known beforehand and constantly under divine control. Even Satan, who inspired Judas to betray him, was in the service of the plan. And so were "the Jews." They were meant to oppose him, to harden their hearts, and eventually even to have him killed. God was as much at work in them, indirectly, as he was in hardening the heart of Pharaoh against the entreaties of Moses to release the Hebrews. And as it happened back then at the point of crisis that released the chosen people and formed them into a single people with a single God, so it happened on the anniversary of that event, the Passover, many hundreds of years later that a similar crisis inaugurated a new stage of consciousness. In these moments of decisive crisis, God shows his glory and his power, leads his people (in twelves) out of bondage, and inaugurates a new stage of consciousness and identity. The pattern is familiar in the biblical narrative.

This is a developmental spiral, passing over the same ground, repeating a pattern, and bringing a new level of spiritual awareness. As John presents this argument, it is in the form of a story about the life and death of Jesus, plus the religious interpretation of this event, and this text is itself then a symbol. As a symbol, the text of the fourth Gospel allows the reader of it to participate in the same inner reality that the author experienced.

As psychological thinkers and reflectors, we interpret this symbol, and in interpreting it we must say something about its meaning in the context of the biblical narrative as a whole. This Gospel account of the life, death, resurrection and meaning of Jesus brings into the light of consciousness a content of the unconscious that had been in preparation for a considerable period of time beforehand. As the image of God, presented throughout the Hebrew Scriptures, had unfolded from Genesis through the Pentateuch, the histories, the prophets, and the Wisdom literature, it had grown and developed in clarity and maturity to the point where this further revelation was possible. The Bible shows a theological thrust, which was later elaborated in Christian Trinitarian theology: first God the Father is revealed, then God the Son, and through the Son and following upon his resurrection, the Holy Spirit. This is not to say that all were not present eternally, from the beginning, but the human perception of

197

them took place historically through various key events and epiphanies.

There has been an evolution in consciousness about the God, Yahweh, who first made Himself known to Moses at the burning bush. John's account of Jesus, his deeds, his words, and the meaning of his human incarnation, adds to what is already known about Yahweh from earlier experiences as recorded in the ancient Hebrew Scriptures. John is not presenting a new god; he is presenting an expanded awareness, in many ways a new awareness, of that same God and what He is like. This new addition to the picture of God importantly alters the portrait of Him and gives the human community essential new information. In this respect, the new image as presented by the author of the Gospel, adds to, and in the process, transforms the previous image.

What does this new symbol show us? First, as stated in the previous lectures, it tells us that this is a God of love and not only one of law and ethics. Jesus represents God as a serving, loving, caring figure. This is a side of God that had certainly been spoken about in the earlier Scriptures, particularly by the prophets in images such as the suffering servant, the good shepherd, and the longsuffering husband, but nowhere has it been so vividly dramatized and so convincingly portrayed. After this revelation of the Divine nature, no one can ever again doubt that God is love. The Gospel symbol of God shows Him as fundamentally and primarily a God of Love who lays down His life for His friends. It also demonstrates that this love, this God, is more powerful than death, the opposing force. Jesus has to die so that he can demonstrate the relativity of death, and in this triumph over death, the God of Love demonstrates his sovereignty.

Love is stronger than death: this is the gospel message. And this is something that was not known before. Certainly there are some indications that death does not conquer all in the Hebrew Scriptures: Enoch is taken to heaven and does not die, as is Elijah, but it is a rule that all die and the notion of an afterlife is not emphasized in the Old Testament. Jesus promises eternal life, tells his followers that they will never die, and himself overcomes death. The risen Christ is a key element of the symbol presented in all four Gospels, especially in the fourth Gospel.

From a rational, common sense point of view, this looks like denial of reality. Everyone dies, including the apostles themselves. Yet the symbol says that those who follow Christ and believe in him will not die and that he conquered death. The fact that believers were still subject to physical death was at first surprising and somewhat scandalizing to the early Christians. Perhaps these believers who died were not really true believers? Perhaps they were at fault and to blame, as we today sometimes blame ourselves or others for getting cancer and other diseases. As if we're not living right!

But the Gospel of John was prepared in some respect for answering this puzzle, because Jesus was clearly speaking in spiritual terms. His dialogue with Nicodemus shows how one can misunderstand his message by taking it too concretely. Being born again? Do you mean entering for a second time into your mother's womb? No, of course not; this is a spiritual birth, a second birth into the spirit. So there is a physical birth and a physical death, and there is a spiritual birth and a spiritual death. What Jesus promises is that his followers will not experience the spiritual death. Their spirits, if they follow the Way, will not die. This is to say that on the spiritual plane of reality, there is no death once one reaches it, and Jesus is the way to reach it. This has been the doctrine of Christians for centuries, and even though the best of Christians have died physically, still the words of Christ that believers will never die continue to console believers, not all of whom are totally irrational and devoid of common sense. It is as though Jesus offered a glimpse into eternity. His words and life and especially his death and resurrection brought into consciousness what had been a dim realization before: that the individual can have contact with eternity and can participate in it. The ego's life is bounded by birth and physical death, by the dawning of personal consciousness in early childhood and its extinction in sleep and old age and death, but at another level, the level of the spirit, we are not so bounded. It was from this perspective that Jesus spoke, as indicated in the records of the Gospel writers, when he spoke of eternal life and of never dying.

When the writer of the fourth Gospel has Jesus say that he is "the gate of the 'sheepfold,'"[93] he is adding a metaphor to the statement that Jesus is the Way. Jesus is speaking to the Pharisees, who, of course, claim that they already have the way (in the Law, in the tradition), and Jesus contradicts them with his claims. Of course, they were not claiming that those who followed them would have eternal life. They did not promise this type of connection to the heavenly realms for the individual, but that is precisely what Jesus was promising: whoever believed in him and followed him as the Way would be personally and individually taken to another level of consciousness and connected to eternity.

Jesus emphasizes repeatedly in the Johannine teachings and discourses that he is the only way, and that only through

---

[93] John 10:7.

him is eternal life possible. The emphatic note of exclusivity is not unknown in the biblical narrative, of course, and Jesus proves himself to be the son of his father in this respect, for Yahweh too is a jealous God who draws the line sharply between those who are of the chosen people and those who are not. This insistence on exclusivity has been responsible for a good deal of the tribalism shown by Christians throughout the ages. The "other" is heathen, unclean, benighted, without grace, etc. The positive value of exclusivity is, however, the creation of strong bonds within the tribal group and a sense of identity on the part of its members. While the new archetype symbolized by Jesus Christ did bring in a new and transformed state of consciousness into the world, and did reveal a new aspect of the God of the Hebrew Scriptures, it also carried forward some of the same patterns and led to a type of tribal structure that was not unknown before. The new chosen people would now displace the old and claim for themselves all the rights and prerogatives that had been enjoyed by the displaced Jews.

On the other hand, Jesus offers the Way and eternal life to anyone who believes in him.

> "Anyone who enters through me will be safe:
> he will go freely in and out
> and be sure of finding pasture."[94]

In this message there is a radical change in the former conditions governing exclusivity. Now, the Way is open to anyone who believes, be they Jew, Samaritan, Greek, Roman, or of any other tribe or nation. Jesus opens the gate to the sheepfold to anyone who will see him as the Way:

---

[94] John 10:9.

> "I am the good shepherd;
> I know my own
> and my own know me,
> just as the Father knows me
> and I know the Father;
> and I lay down my life for my sheep.
> And there are other sheep I have
> that are not of this fold,
> and these I have to lead as well.
> They too will listen to my voice,
> and there will be only one flock,
> and one shepherd."[95]

The author places an emphasis here on universalism and on individual response: You may belong to any flock, to any nation or group, and if you personally see Christ as the Way, then you may be included among his own and he will recognize you and protect you. He becomes for you, too, the good shepherd.

Who are these that can see? Why do some see and others not? Why are some drawn to this Way and others put off by it or left cold? There must be some predisposition to respond to the symbol of Christ before one has ever actually seen it or been exposed to it. There are some who just "see," no matter their background or heritage. Psychologically, we would suppose that the archetype represented by Christ is already sort of half constellated in their psyches. They are already spiritual people potentially and only need a concrete figure on which to project the symbol of the self. Their souls are Christ-like before they ever know Christ. When such a

---

[95] John 10:14-16.

person hears the stories about Jesus, or reads a text such as John's Gospel, which is a brilliant presentation of the symbol, they find themselves drawn to it. This is what they have been searching for without knowing it; this is what they hungered for and thirsted after without knowing how to satisfy their spiritual needs. These are those whose souls are fertile ground for the seed of the gospel. They can make an immediate identification with Christ for they are themselves unconsciously Christ-like. The Christ within matches up with the Christ without.

Is every human soul potentially Christ-like? Are we all Christian at some unconscious level? Probably so, since the archetypes are universal and belong to the general human inventory. But in the same breath we would have to say that the Christ archetype is not the only one, and that some people are much more strongly governed and constellated in their consciousness by other archetypes. In Greek religion, you could take your pick among several temples: Aphrodite, Zeus, Apollo, Hera, etc., and depending upon your tendencies and preferences and psychological constellation, you would gravitate more to one than another. Tradition and culture also, of course, play a strong influence on choice of spirituality. One can also combine various archetypal patterns and images. For instance, the Japanese today will typically visit Buddhist temples, Shinto shrines, and even Christian churches without apparent inner contradiction. Each has its own value – its own meaning and purpose. But in the Judeo-Christian biblical tradition, God is a jealous God and does not go in for this kind of tolerance of a variety of archetypal patterns. This would be seen as infidelity. And in Jesus' words, as spoken in the various discourses of the

fourth Gospel, we find a strong emphasis on exclusivity of
the bond to him:

"I am the vine,
you are the branches.
Whoever remains in me, with me in him,
bears fruit in plenty;
for cut off from me you can do nothing.
Anyone who does not remain in me
is like a branch that has been thrown away
- he withers;
these branches are collected and thrown on the fire,
and they are burnt."[96]

This strong emphasis on exclusiveness and tight
bonding to Jesus as the one and only Way would present a
critical problem in the early church when it came to issues
of discernment among various possible interpretations and
versions of the gospel. Whose teachings could be accepted
as true and legitimate once Jesus was no longer around to
validate them? What is the right opinion (i.e., "orthodox")?
The early followers who were left behind when Jesus
ascended to heaven were plagued by this problem. Jesus had
said he was sending the Holy Spirit (called "the Advocate")
after him and this "person" would continue teaching them.
In fact, one of the reasons Jesus had to leave, he said, was so
that the Advocate could come. As long as he was here in the
flesh, the Holy Spirit was held off, but when Jesus departed
and returned to the Father, then this figure would be free to
come and dwell among them:

---

[96] John 15:5-6.

"Still, I must tell you the truth:
it is for your own good that I am going
because unless I go,
the Advocate will not come to you;
but if I do go,
I will send him to you.
And when he comes,
he will show the world how wrong it was...
But when the Spirit of truth comes
he will lead you to the complete truth,
since he will not be speaking as from himself
but will say only what he has learnt;
and he will tell you of the things to come."[97]

So, on the one hand Jesus insists on exclusivity as the Way, the Truth, and the Life, and indeed also gives his disciples the power to forgive and to retain sins (John 20:23) and to carry forward his work of presenting the Way to the world; but on the other hand, the Holy Spirit is unleashed by his leaving, and this creates the possibility of various people claiming that they are speaking from divine inspiration. How is one to discern the truth among various versions and claims?

One line of possible development was taken by the so-called Gnostics. These were, in part at least, spiritual individuals who responded to the symbol of Christ inwardly and claimed to be taught further spiritual truths by the Holy Spirit who had come to dwell in them. Sometimes their visions and the teachings they claimed to have learned from these visionary dialogues departed considerably from the mainstream of teaching as put forward by the apostles and their developing tradition of belief. Irenaeus claimed that

---

[97] John 16:7-8;13.

each individual Gnostic had his or her own religious/ mythological system based on individual revelations. He found this distasteful in the extreme and excoriated the Gnostics for this kind of wanton pluralism. The orthodox tradition formed around debates like these, gradually deciding through the formation of a canon of sacred texts and through creeds and authoritative teachings and offices what would be considered true opinion and what heresy.

Uniformity of teaching and belief was the goal and became the result to a considerable extent. This represents a consolidation of the new attitude represented by Jesus and the writers of the Gospels and other New Testament texts. In time, this became as fixed and doctrinaire as the attitude it had replaced, which in the fourth Gospel is so starkly represented by "the Jews." The Gnostics, who lost the struggle, were buried in the sands of history, and it was only in the 20th Century, in Egypt, in 1945, that some of their writings were discovered. It is interesting, historically, that this recovery of Gnostic texts corresponded almost exactly to the Jews recovery of their homeland after a similarly long period.

The Gnostic option, had it prevailed, would have led presumably to a much more pluralistic and individual type of religious culture. Spiritual life was based on the individual's experience of a vision, of a revelatory figure, and of what we would call today a content of the unconscious. Sometimes these figures would have corresponded to the traditional images of Christ, the Father, etc., but sometimes not. There would have been an individual difference. There would have been a greater reliance on the working of the Holy Spirit in the individual rather than only in and through the structures of the established church as controlled by ordained bishops. In a way, the Protestant Reformation took up this individualistic option, loosening the tie between the individual and the collective and placing more stress on personal access to God through prayer and less on the sacramental means of grace. In our own day, psychotherapy, as pointed out by Elaine Pagels in her book, *The Gnostic Gospels*, has taken up the Gnostic approach in its emphasis on individual self-discovery and exploration without reference to orthodox creeds of belief. Jung's practice of active imagination was, for him and for the tradition of practice following him, a means for contacting the spirit of the unconscious and for searching out the transcendent function in the individual psyche. On a secular level, this is an exact parallel to the Gnostic search for the living Christ within. Jung's *Red Book* is a testimonial to the efficacy of this practice.

As I argued in the previous lecture, a psychological interpretation of the Christ symbol as portrayed in the fourth Gospel shows it to be a representation of what in Jungian psychology is called the transcendent function. This is the Way, the door, the bridge between conscious and un-conscious, between time and eternity, between ego and self. To find this psychic factor within as a living spiritual presence gives the individual access to the eternal realms of the archetypes as well as comfort in the perspective that the ego's limitations of time and knowledge are not the ultimate definitions of human life. As an example of this perspective, the following quote from the opening of Jung's auto-biography is instructive:

> "Life has always seemed to me like a plant that lives on its rhizome. Its true life is invisible, hidden in the rhizome. The part that appears above ground lasts only a single summer. Then it withers away – an ephemeral apparition. When we think of the unending growth and decay of life and

civilizations, we cannot escape the impression of absolute nullity. Yet I have never lost a sense of something that lives and endures underneath the eternal flux. What we see is the blossom, which passes. The rhizome remains.

In the end the only events in my life worth telling are those when the imperishable world erupted into this transitory one. That is why I speak chiefly of inner experiences, amongst which I include my dreams and visions."[98]

If you read Jung's autobiography carefully for religious experiences – visions, dreams, intuitions – it is evident that many belong in the mainstream of the Judeo-Christian tradition, and among them are important images of Christ himself. When Jung agreed with Tertullian that the soul is naturally Christian, he was speaking for himself from his own inner experience.

The fourth Gospel gives us a picture of Christ as the Way. He comes from the heavenly realms of glory, pitches his tent among us for a time, teaches, creates an intense bond of love with his own, suffers death as a part of the divine plan so that he can demonstrate his power over it, and returns to the realms of glory, leaving behind the Holy Spirit to further teach and guide. Set in the context of the biblical narrative, this is a new revelation of God and an opening of a new Way to access and fellowship with Him. The image of Yahweh is transformed from Master and Law-giver and distant King into loving Father. Through the image of Christ, human consciousness discovers Love as belonging to its own essential nature and perhaps to the essential nature of all that is.

---

[98] C.G. Jung, *Memories, Dreams, Reflections* (New York: Vintage Books, 1961), 4.

Bibliography

Brown, Raymond (1970) *The Gospel According to John: The Anchor Bible,* New York, London: Doubleday.

Freud, Sigmund, (1939) "Moses Was an Egyptian," in *Moses and Monotheism*, London: Hogarth Press.

Jung, C.G., (1955/1970) *Mysterium Coniunctionis* (H. Read, M. Fordham, G. Adler Eds.), *The Collected Works of C.G. Jung*, vol. 14, Princeton: Princeton University Press.

_____ (1961/1989) *Memories, Dreams, Reflections*, recorded and edited by A. Jaffé, New York: Vintage Books.

_____ (1968) Aion: *Researches into the phenomenology of the self* (R. F. C. Hull, Trans.) (H. Read et al., Eds.), *The Collected Works of C.G. Jung,* Vol. 9ii, 2nd ed., Princeton: Princeton University Press. (Original work published 1951).

_____ (1969) *Answer to Job, The Collected Works of C.G. Jung,* Vol. 11, Princeton: Princeton University Press.

_____ (1977) *C.G. Jung Speaking: Interviews and Encounters*, William McGuire and R.F.C. Hull (eds.) Princeton, NJ: Princeton University Press.

Kluger, Rivkah (1974) "The Idea of the Chosen People in the Old Testament: A Contribution to the Symbolism of Individuation," in *Psyche and Bible*, New York: Spring Publications, pp. 3-43.

_____ (1967) "Satan as Independent Demon," in *Satan in the Old Testament*, Evanston, IL: Northwestern University Press, pp. 149-162.